SPELLING

RESOURCE

BOOK

Particular contributors to the Spelling: Resource Book include:
- Diana Rees, Education Department of Western Australia,
- Kay Kovalevs, Education Department of Western Australia,
- Alison Dewsbury, Education Department of Western Australia.

First Steps was developed by the Education Department of Western Australia under the direction of Alison Dewsbury.

Longman Australia Pty Limited
Longman House
Kings Gardens
95 Coventry Street
Melbourne 3205 Australia

Offices in Sydney, Brisbane and Perth, and associated
companies throughout the world.

Published by Longman Australia on behalf of the
Education Department of Western Australia.

Designed by Kikitsa Michalantos
Produced by Longman Australia Pty Ltd
Printed in Malaysia through Longman Malaysia, PA

National Library of Australia
Cataloguing-in-Publication data

Spelling: resource book.

ISBN 0 582 91570 8.

1. English language - Orthography and spelling - Study
and teaching (Primary). 2. Language arts (Primary). I.
Western Australia. Education Dept. (Series: First steps
(Perth, W.A.)).

372.632044.

Contents

Appendices

Chapter 1:

First Steps Spelling in the Classroom

Introduction

It is recognised that communication occurs when a writer has effectively relayed his or her meaning to the reader. Good spelling is a factor in effectively relaying meaning. The First Steps *Spelling: Resource Book* complements the *Spelling: Developmental Continuum* by providing teachers with additional ideas for developing proficient spellers.

This opening chapter suggests that as a first step towards building competence in spelling, teachers create a classroom environment which encourages risk-taking and having-a-go in spelling while maintaining fluency in writing. Later chapters describe specific strategies such as use of a spelling journal, understanding graphophonics (sound-symbol) relationships through the activity 'Sound Sleuth', and studying words through word origins. Direct references are made to such strategies in the *Spelling: Developmental Continuum*. In chapters 5 and 6 assessment and evaluation ideas, and strategies for helping children who are experiencing problems with spelling are respectively provided. Additional resources such as photocopiable prompt cards are located amongst the Appendices.

The Role of the Teacher

The teacher provides:

- a classroom climate which fosters learning
- a classroom environment which supports children's learning
- a wide variety of resources which support children's learning
- activities and strategies appropriate to children's phase of development
- modelling and support for children as they develop effective strategies

Classroom Climate

The teacher creates a classroom climate that is warm and positive. Risk-taking and 'having a go' are highly prized. Children know that their efforts are valued. They are given credit for problem-solving and for using available resources, both human and material. They are encouraged to be reflective learners who are responsible for their own learning, but who work interactively, sharing their discoveries with others. Cooperation, trust, challenge and encouragement characterise the classroom.

Inclusion of the following elements ensures that successful learning takes place:

P • the children should be involved in *problem solving*
E • problems should be *embedded* in real life contexts
W • *working memory* should be taken into account
I • they should have the opportunities to *interact* with each other and adults
T • children should have *time* to practise and internalise what they learn

Children need to be given structured time to:

R • Reflect on what they are learning
R • Represent what they are learning in a concrete form
R • Report on what they have learned to the teacher and to each other

Classroom Environment

A Print-rich Environment

The classroom environment is full of print which is relevant, topical, useful and attractive. It is presented in natural and meaningful contexts. It is important that print is displayed where children can read it and use it effectively. Teachers provide labels, signs, descriptions on murals, charts of poems, lists of known songs, instructions, helpers rosters, timetables, banks of words and class writing. Children can be involved in the preparation of the print and encouraged to add to it and use it whenever possible, e.g. children can search for examples of words with a common letter pattern and develop a class chart. Teachers constantly make use of environmental print for focusing on particular aspects of language.

Class Writing Centre

The Writing Centre includes a variety of writing and publishing materials, interesting messages, work samples, a writing ideas box, dictionaries and examples of different forms of writing, e.g. letters, notes, lists, reports and pamphlets.

Class Reading Corner

An attractive Reading Corner is established where children's favourite books are always available. It is important to include a range of different genre, books by the same author, children's book reviews, class-made books and work samples from class reading activities.

Classroom Resources

The following print resources provide children with a means of tracking down a word they wish to use by looking for it in a text which they have helped to write; a chart which they have helped to create; or a reference book they have been taught to use.

Class Books

Class books of various kinds can be developed with the children. These books can demonstrate any genre and be related to any curriculum area, e.g.

– Maths (writing about different shapes found in the class or how to make a sundial)
– Science (writing about human made/natural objects, or keeping guinea pigs)
– Music (writing about sounds in the environment, school, home, playground, park or pool)
– General (writing about excursions, text innovations, narratives, reports, jokes or riddles)

Our class guinea pigs are called 'Snorty' and 'Patchy.'

They like to eat guinea pig pellets, cabbage leaves and carrots.

Class Diary

Class diaries can be used for modelled writing, or collaborative and individual writing. The diary can be presented in different forms, e.g. 'big book', charts, as a calendar.

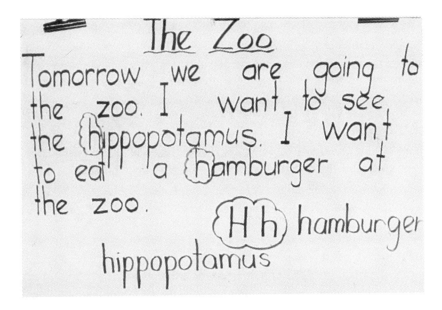

Word Banks

Word banks are developed that relate to class topics, common English letter patterns, high frequency words, words with a similar meaning base, visual patterns, sound patterns and spelling generalisations. Children need to take part in developing these word banks so they are meaningful to them.

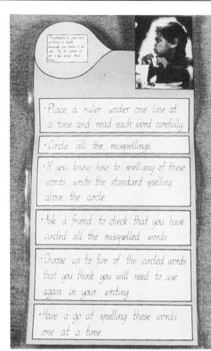

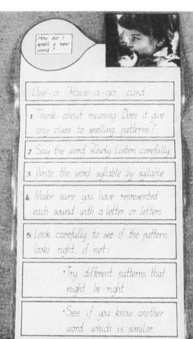

Spelling Charts

The most important chart in the room is that which is being created by the children as an outcome of their Reflection, Representation and Reporting sessions. These are described in *Spelling: Developmental Continuum* (see pages 36, 52, 71, 91 and 106 of that book). It is on this chart that children's discoveries are recorded after they have been shared with the class. The chart serves three purposes:

– it gives value and status to children's discoveries
– it helps children see where their current discoveries fit into the overall spelling system
– it serves as a record for the teacher of what children actually know

Reference Books

It is important to ensure that there is a variety of resources available for checking spelling, e.g. commercial dictionaries, thesauruses, resource books, children's self - made dictionaries. Children know what resources are available and have a clear understanding of how they should be used. Resources need to be readily accessible.

Have-a-Go Pads

'Have-a-go' pads provide children with the opportunity to try out their ideas and build on previous attempts. After drafting and revising their writing, children are encouraged to put a line under any words they feel may not be correct and then have another go in their 'have-a-go' pads. Teachers may then write the word beside the child's attempts. Children compare their spelling with the correct version and rewrite the word if incorrect. Words from the 'have-a-go' pad may be included in the child's spelling journal (see diagram on page 14).

Spelling Journals

The introduction of spelling journals into the class helps to individualise spelling on the basis of children's writing needs. Words to be included in the child's journal can come from any writing they have done across the different curriculum areas. Teachers may also include class focus words, high frequency words, interest words and subject-specific words. Chapter 2 of this book beginning on page 11 explains the use of spelling journals in the writing program.

Activities and Strategies

These can be found listed according to phase of development in the chapters entitled 'Teaching Graphophonics' (page 40) and 'Word Study and Proof Reading' (page 53).

Modelling and Support

It is important to model specific strategies and processes to support children's development as they move through the different phases of spelling.

Specific Strategies and Processes that can be modelled during Language sessions

Preliminary Speller	Semi-Phonetic Speller	Phonetic Speller	Transitional Speller	Independent Speller
Conventional spelling during 'Modelled Writing'	→	→	→	→
'Having-a-go' - during 'Modelled Writing'	→	→	→	→
	Sounding out when 'having-a-go' at a word	Identifying sound-symbol relationships	→	→
	Finding words around the room	Identifying common visual patterns	→	→
	Identifying sound-symbol relationships in context	Identifying critical features of words	→	→
	Noticing similarities and differences between words	A process for learning words: Look. Cover. Write. Check.	→	→
		Use of 'have-a-go' pads	→	→
	Use of personal dictionary	*Use of a spelling journal*	→	→
		Proof-reading work. Underlining words they think may not be correct	→	Different proof-reading skills
		→ Generating alternative spellings	→ Process for trying to write new words	→
			Use of meaning as a strategy	
		Use of spelling resources	→	

Teaching Children Spelling Strategies

Developing Confident and Effective Spellers

Learning about words is an individual process, all children need to:

- build their own lists of words and learn them
- know how to learn difficult words
- have easy access to correct spelling models
- construct an understanding of and ability to use spelling rules
- build specific-interest, subject related and vocabulary extension lists
- explore language and play with words to increase their knowledge about words
- discover rules and definitions for themselves through problem solving
- accept responsibility for their own learning. This includes learning to spell correctly
- be involved in open-ended activities so that they can work at their own level of competency
- have fun when learning how language works

To become proficient spellers, children need to

- Be encouraged to take risks in spelling and 'have a go' at spelling words they are unsure of, while maintaining fluency in writing. The following chart of suggestions makes a useful reference in the classroom, or can be used as a display on children's desks. It is important that teachers model the techniques often so that children become aware of them.

What to do if you can't spell a word

Guess	put a line under the word or circle it and check the spelling later
Write	as much as you can of the word and fill in the details later, e.g. *bec—s* (because)
Syllabify	tap out the syllables, saying them quietly, then write the word bit by bit, e.g. *yes/ter/day*
Write	the word several ways and choose the one that looks right, e.g. *lern*, *learn*, *lurn*
Ask	someone
Refer	to chart, class lists, books around the room
Use	a dictionary

- Become aware of the techniques that proficient spellers use to learn words. Some useful ways to learn a word include:

(i) **Look** - focus on the part you don't know
   Cover - cover the word
   Write - write it from memory
   Check - check the spelling

   Model this strategy using some means such as a fold-back blackboard, a chart with cover strip, or a teacher-made or commercial spelling folder.

(ii) **Look at** and identify the critical parts and features bec(au)se

(iii) **Fill the gap**

Write the following pattern three times for each word and have the student fill in the gaps. Once children are familiar with the technique they can make up their own patterns.

school	school	school
schoo_	schoo_	schoo_
scho__	scho__	scho__
sch___	sch___	sch___
sc____	sc____	sc____
s_____	s_____	s_____
_____	_____	_____

(iv) **Mnemonics**

Proficient spellers often use memory tricks and rules to help them remember difficult words:

Only 'E's are buried in the cemetery.
I before E except after C, when the word rhymes with Key.
'Mediterranean' has terra (earth) in it so it's double 'r', not double 't'.
My pal is the principal.
A piece of pie.
You fri the end of your friend.
Never end a friendship.
You hear with your ears.
Parallel has 3 parallel lines.
Place names all have here in them—here, there, where and everywhere.
Take a bus to your business.
Never believe a lie.
Question openers begin with wh—who, where, what, when, why.
Is is a verb and so is practise.
Ice is a noun and so is practice.
The fourth number in four.
An island is land.
Affect has an a for action.
The two twins are twenty.
Too has another o as well as to.
Necessary has one collar and two socks.
A special agent is someone in the CIA.
Don't let the cat catch the mouse.
Separate has 'a rat' in it.
Saturday is the day you are (u r) glad to see come each week.
Lions eat meat.
Loose tooth.
In a diary you write about yourself so *i* comes first.
If you buy it you bought it.
If you bring it you brought it.
You can hear your heart.
You can sign a sign.

Encourage children to create their own mnemonics and share their ideas with others.

9

- Learn to use a variety of sources to find correct spelling. The classroom needs to be full of print that the children have helped to produce, e.g. favourite quotes, word banks, poems, children's writing, charts of word discoveries — homophones, acronyms, synonyms and so on. It is also most useful to have several different types of dictionaries including those that refer to roots and derivatives. Children can then use different dictionaries for different purposes.
- Understand that spelling needs to be checked at a later date.
- Develop proof reading skills
- Learn to use a Have-a-Go pad
- Learn to use a Spelling Journal

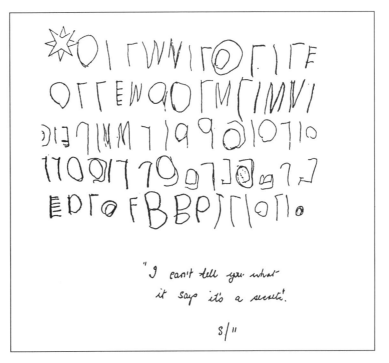

I can't tell you what it says - it's a secret. (Preliminary Spelling sample)

Rosa was in the cafe. Rosa jumped on the chair. (Semi-Phonetic Spelling sample)

Chapter 2:

Using a Spelling Journal in the Writing Program

Introduction

This section describes how a spelling journal can be used to individualise spelling on the basis of children's writing needs. A spelling journal can be easily incorporated into the language program, providing opportunities for children of all ability levels to take responsibility for their own learning.

It is important to note that for those children experiencing difficulty with spelling, use of a journal makes spelling more meaningful, as they become involved in selecting and learning words from their own writing. Working with a spelling journal is less threatening for children than more traditional approaches to spelling. Children test each other on their personal list of words and then record the results in their journals. They have the opportunity to set personal goals and work towards achieving these at their own rate, without any fear of comparisons being made. A consequence of this is that self-esteem is enhanced and children become more independent spellers.

Specific aspects of class organisation and management that need to be considered are also identified before a spelling journal is incorporated into the language program. Specific demonstrations teachers need to plan and implement to ensure that children develop the skills and strategies needed for language control are also described.

What is a Spelling Journal?

Purpose

The purpose of a spelling journal is to individualise spelling on the basis of children's writing needs.

Children are involved in working with:
    words misspelt in their writing,
    class focus words,
    subject-specific words, and
    interest words.

Personal spelling journals provide children with the opportunity to take responsibility for their own spelling needs. They learn spelling strategies, develop problem-solving strategies, develop understanding of important processes and become involved in collaborative learning.

Features

A spelling journal provides space for children to write:

- words that they have misspelt in their writing, and key features of those words to help remember them correctly

Word	Key Features	Tests 1	2	3	4	5	T
dissatisfaction	dis/satisfaction						
faithfully	faithful/ly						
geography	geo (earth)						
receive	receive						

- mnemonics and spelling hints

Mnemonics and Spelling Hints
Parallel has three parallel lines
Piece of pie
My pal is the principal

- subject-specific words that they need to be able to spell
- words that are personally significant

Subject-Specific Words

Social Studies	English
economic, plateau	rhyme, anthology
Maths	Home Economics
diameter, forty	cereal, dining

- personal evaluation comments about spelling development and achievement of individual goals

Last week I was able to cross five words off my list. I am having difficulty learning to spell accommodation and plateau but I was able to use a mnemonic to help me learn to spell parallel.

Other pages that invite children to focus on prefixes, suffixes, homophones, homographs and Latin and Greek derivations may be included.

The Latin Influence

Latin Root	Meaning	Examples
scribo scribere scripsi scriptum	write	scribble describe. manuscript scripture prescription

How a Journal is Used

A spelling journal is used as a part of a language program. Children are encouraged to select words to learn from their writing. They are shown how to learn words using 'Look, Cover, Write, Check' strategies. When studying words key features provide a major focus. Emphasis is placed on children recognising and learning the key patterns within words they have had difficulty in spelling.

Time is provided during the language program for children to learn their words and then test each other.

Focus on Children

Before introducing a spelling journal into the classroom, teachers need to ensure that children are aware of the particular processes and strategies related to 'having-a-go' and learning words. Children need to understand that writing is an important means of communication and that correct spelling enhances this communication, and is an expectation when writing for particular audiences and purposes.

To ensure that a spelling journal is meaningful and useful to children, teachers need to provide opportunities for children to be:

- involved in a stimulating and meaningful writing program
- writing every day for different audiences and purposes across the curriculum
- given the opportunity to draft, revise, edit, proof read and share their writing
- willing to experiment, solve problems and think of alternatives
- aware of the 'have-a-go' strategy and be using 'have-a-go' pads as an integral part of he writing process
- aware of different spelling strategies (graphophonic relationships, visual patterns, meaning based relationships)
- aware of a process for learning new or difficult words
- able to proof read their work by underlining words in their writing that may not be correct
- able to work cooperatively with a partner. Children need to be supported in developing cooperative learning skills through small group and partner work. These skills need to be taught, practised and then feedback should be given on how well the skills were used
- aware of the features of text that has achieved its purpose

13

The following diagram represents the 'have-a-go' process and shows the relationship between children's writing and 'have-a-go' pads, and 'have-a-go pads' and spelling journals.

Having-a-go

Children's Draft Writing

Onse <u>apon</u> a time
<u>ther</u> was a <u>locing</u>
vampire he livd next
to me. won nght I
had to <u>yos</u> his telefon
to ring my mome and
dad up it had al spidr
webs on it he <u>gav</u> me
a cup <u>ov</u> cofy I chued
it <u>awa</u>

Children underline any words they think are not correct and then select three to five words to try again in their 'have-a-go' pads.

'Have-a-go' Pad

1st Try	2nd Try	Correct Spelling
gaiv	gave ✓	
yoos	yoose	use
theer	their	there
ove	ovve	of
upon ✓		

Children have two attemps at the work and tick the one they believe to be correct. Spelling attempts are then checked by the teacher, or children may use a dictionary.

A Spelling Journal

Word	Key features	Tests 1 2 3 4 5
use	use	
of		
there	there	

Children select words they need to learn from their 'have-a-go' pads. These words are written into their spelling journals.

Focus on Teachers

Use of a spelling journal should become a natural part of the class language program. Teachers need to allow time for children to select, learn, partner-test their words and then talk about their work with teacher and peers.

Planned Demonstrations

Teacher demonstrations are an important part of all language sessions. During these demonstrations children become aware of important strategies used and decisions made by writers in the composing process. Teachers need to employ 'think aloud' strategies to demonstrate how successful writers problem-solve.

Teachers can plan demonstrations to meet the needs of all children in the class. This may involve modelling different strategies and processes with the whole class or a small group.

Teachers may need to model:
• the 'have-a-go' process
• identification of key features of words
• a process for trying to write new words
• a process for remembering commonly misspelt words
• proof reading
• meaning-based strategies

Management of a Spelling Journal

As the use of a spelling journal encourages responsibility and independence, teachers may need to review their role, identifying where their support is needed the most.

Teachers need to:

- Establish what the role of the teacher will be, i.e. observing, guiding, conferencing, listening, discussing, encouraging, providing opportunities, modelling strategies and processes
- Plan how the use of a spelling journal will be incorporated into the class language program. Decisions will be based on the children's needs.

  When deciding how the use of a spelling journal will be incorporated into the class language program, it is important to take into account the purpose of a spelling journal and its important link with the writing program. A decision needs to be made on how a spelling journal will be introduced as a whole class strategy and later further developed and refined to meet individual and group needs.

  Use of a spelling journal in a classroom will depend very much on teaching style and the needs of the particular group of children with which a teacher is working. A number of accounts of different teacher management and organisational procedures are included in this book beginning on page 22.

- Decide on the format of spelling journal. It is worthwhile examining different examples of spelling journals and developing a format that is appropriate for a particular group of children.

Introducing the Use of a Spelling Journal Into the Classroom

Step 1   *Discuss with children the aim of the spelling journal.*

A spelling journal is used to:

record words from writing with which you are having difficulty

provide a process that links spelling with writing

develop a bank of words that you can use when writing

collect interesting words, class focus words, topic related words

build up lists of words you know how to spell

Step 2   *Discuss how children will choose words to go into their journal.*

Words chosen will be those children are using but misspelling in their written work, although not every word that is misspelled has to be included. The words can come from any writing that takes place throughout the day, e.g. language experience, diary writing, recounts, narratives, reading activities, science reports, social studies notes, written answers in maths.

Children need to understand that there will be some negotiation of words that are to be included. It is important that students have a chance to select those words that they want *to learn as well as the teacher indicating words that the students* need *to learn.*

Step 3   *Discuss when words should be entered into journals.*

Children are provided with 'have-a-go' pads. These pads are kept on their desk so words can be added at any time throughout the day. Some of these words are then copied into the 'Words to Learn' section of the journal at a set time each day.

Children need to check spelling of words they are entering with peers, the teacher or other word sources. Teachers need to carry out frequent checks on the accuracy of words copied into the journal.

Step 4   *Model the process of selecting words to enter into a spelling journal.*

Children are shown how words are selected from personal writing, 'have-a-go' pad and class focus list, then written into their journal, highlighting key features.

It is important to note that initially some children may need teacher support when doing this. Children who make lots of spelling errors in their written work need to be encouraged to select just two or three 'common usage' words to focus on.

Step 5   Discuss how to learn the words.

Show children how they will begin; by studying and learning the first two to five words at the top of their *Words to Learn* list.

Time will be given before partner-testing for children to learn the words. Children should be reminded of the different strategies they know to help with learning words, e.g. 'Look, Cover, Write, Check', focusing on key features, using mnemonics, identifying critical features, looking for visual patterns and meaning relationships.

After partner-testing all work is marked by the teacher and children record their results in their journals.

As a child achieves three consecutive ticks for a word (i.e. the word is correct when tested on three consecutive days) then the word is ruled through. The child then adds the next word from his/her list for study and testing. The core of two to five words is always maintained. If the child *does not* get three consecutive ticks for a word and has been tested on it five times, then a *T* for transfer is printed in the *T* column, and the word is placed at the end of the entire list of words to learn, for further study at a later time.

Step 6   Explain partner-testing and recording procedures.

It is recommended that children study up to five words a day to start with and are 'partner-tested' on these. This is a manageable number of words and it means that all the partner-testing can be dealt with in approximately 10 minutes each day.

Each child has a special mini-pad in which to write their words. The following procedure is recommended when introducing a spelling journal to the whole class.

1 When children are confident that they know the words in their lists, each child takes a partner.
2 Each partner tests the list of five words.
3 Completed tests are placed in the **IN** tray on teacher's desk.
4 Teacher marks tests throughout the session.
5 Marked tests are placed in the **OUT** tray for distribution.
6 Children collect pads that have been marked and distribute them as they return to their seats.
7 Remaining partner is tested in the same way and the process is repeated.
8 Results are recorded by a tick or cross.
9 Any words with three consecutive ticks are crossed off the list, in pencil.
10 New words are added to bring the list up to the required number.

Step 7   Discuss self evaluation strategies and student– teacher conferences.

At the end of the week children are asked to review their spelling journal work and record in their journals comments relating to successes or problems. They should also be encouraged to set goals for the following week. Children are asked to share these self-evaluations during student-teacher conferences.

Step 8   Discuss the importance of legibility.

Children need to understand the importance of writing their words clearly so they are easy for their partner to read and their teacher to check.

Step 9   Discuss entering words that are homophones.

When homophones are misspelt, e.g. there/their, the entire phrase should be written down, e.g. 'their books'. This is to ensure that the correct word is studied and tested.

Use of a spelling journal can be incorporated into the language program in many different ways. A number of accounts of different teachers' organisational procedures are included at the end of this chapter.

While organisational features may vary from teacher to teacher the purpose of a spelling journal should be kept clearly in mind, i.e. *to individualise spelling on the basis of children's writing needs.*

Sample Lesson Incorporating the Use of Spelling Journals

The following example of a language session incorporating working with a spelling journal has been included as a suggestion of how to begin using a spelling journal in the classroom.

Step 1 (Whole Class Activity)
Teacher and children work through a planned whole class language activity, e.g. shared book, modelled writing, language experience, word study. Following this the related task will be discussed, e.g. word sorting, sequencing text, written cloze, text innovation, a character profile or story map. This task will be completed later in the lesson after partner testing.

Step 2 (Individual Activity)
Children are given time to study and learn words from their spelling journal before they are tested. Children are reminded about strategies for learning words.

Step 3 (Partner Activity)
Partner testing, as described on Page 17.

Step 4 (Individual Activity)
Children record results and proceed with the nominated language activity.

Step 5 (Group Activity)
Teacher works with small groups of children or individuals. Groups are formed on a needs basis. Special focus groups may be formed to work on any of the following: developing a high frequency vocabulary, developing visual strategies, examining groups of words and making generalisations, developing proof reading skills, playing with language, teacher modelling of spelling strategies, word investigation or writing activities.

Step 6 (Whole Class Activity)
Whole class sharing. Class comes back together to discuss aspects of the work completed in the session. Children may, on occasions, be involved in self-evaluation, i.e. children write in their journals about how their spelling is going and may set themselves some goals for the next week or month.

Note:
This particular session may take place two or three times a week with the whole class. This is very much a whole class approach. Any other needs in relation to spelling could be accommodated within the context of the reading and writing program.

Questions Frequently Asked by Teachers

1 How can a journal incorporate lists, yet still be individualised?

This can be achieved by pre-testing list words and having children enter any errors they make into their journal, along with words from their writing.

2 How does the use of a spelling journal reflect whole language teaching principles?

Very well, as writing provides the context for focusing on spelling. Children have control over their own learning as they select words from their writing to enter into personal spelling journals. Any time spent on learning words is meaningful, as the words chosen are words the child is using in his or her writing.

3 What about weak spellers who really lack confidence when it comes to spelling and make lots of errors in their written work?

It is important not to overload the weaker speller. These children will need some teacher support in selecting words to learn and it may be necessary to limit the number of words they choose from their writing to two or three. It is important to remember that the purpose of a spelling journal is to individualise spelling on the basis of children's writing needs. Therefore children are able to work at their own rate, with a manageable list of words. Weaker children benefit from this approach because they are not involved in whole class testing where comparisons are made.

4 What about reluctant writers, children who aren't interested in writing and write very little so few words are generated?

For journal use to be really effective, children need to be generating lots of writing, so it is important to identify strategies that support reluctant writers. A number of different strategies are described beginning on page 90 of this book. All of these strategies are effective and should lead to increased interest and output from writers as they participate in authentic writing activities.

5 What should I do about children who are very good spellers and make few errors in their writing?

Again, it is important to keep in mind the purpose of a spelling journal (individualising spelling on the basis of children's writing needs). Good spellers may not need to use a journal as frequently as weaker spellers, however, journal use should encompass an extension and enrichment function. It is important to be flexible about how a journal is used, so after introducing it to the whole class, usage should be adapted to meet the needs of individuals and groups. As a consequence of this, it could be that some children in the class will be involved in partner testing three or four times a week while other children may test each other less frequently.

6 How do I ensure children are learning a wide range of words?

To ensure that a wide range of words is being used, it is important to monitor word usage in children's writing. Attention needs to be focused on the development of word knowledge, varied vocabulary and range of words from across the different curriculum areas. Teacher input in relation to class focus words, high frequency words, interest words, is also important.

7 What about testing? I am required to send home fortnightly tests which include a list of twenty words.

If this is a non-negotiable situation you can ask children to partner test each other on, for example, every second or fourth word that has been crossed off in their spelling journal. This can then be marked and evaluated by the teacher. An alternative to this is to send home 'work samples' that really show the development of children's spelling skills in their writing. This can be accompanied by comments from the child and the teacher relating to aspects of the writing task.

8 How do I know if children are achieving? At least with lists I know exactly what words the children know and don't know.

There is a lot of evidence to suggest that knowledge of words in lists isn't always transferred to children's writing. So we can't assume that just because a child gets a word correct in 'list work' that it is known. The real evidence of children's knowledge and understanding of words can be gained by looking at the words they are using in their writing and recording in their spelling journals. Words used correctly provide evidence of a child's growing bank of known words, while non-standard spellings indicate awareness of common spelling patterns, sound/symbol relationships, meaning relationships and the strategies they are using when 'having a go' at words. The *Spelling: Developmental Continuum* provides a framework for gathering detailed information about children's developing knowledge skills and understandings.

9 How do you ensure that words are written correctly into children's journals?

Unfortunately there is no easy answer to this question. It is *critical* that words are written into the journal correctly before children spend time learning them. As a consequence of this, most teachers personally check all words children enter into their journals. This can be done relatively quickly if children leave their books open on their desks or in a special spelling box before they go out to recess.

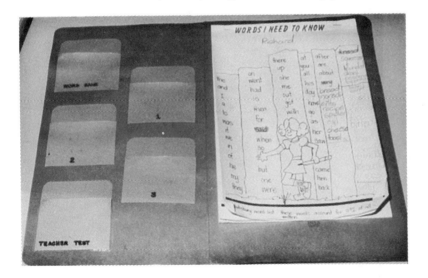

Specific Examples of Organisational Procedures

To assist teacher understanding of use of spelling journals, we asked a number of teachers to describe how they use journals in their class language program. We have included examples from Upper, Middle and Junior Primary teachers from a range of schools in different localities.

It is interesting to examine the different ways teachers have adapted use of a spelling journal to meet the needs of the particular group of children with which they are working. We see that while the intentions of a spelling journal always remain the same, management and organisational aspects can be adapted to suit each teaching/learning situation.

We gratefully acknowledge the contributrions made by the following teachers.

Maxine Shortland-Jones

Jenny Snell

Judy Hayden

Annette Edwards-Parker

Heather Jolly

Paul Stein

Chris Leed

Example 1

Teacher: Maxine Shortland-Jones

Class: Year 1 (five and six year olds)

Using Spelling Journals in a Year 1 Classroom

I have a regular Year 1 class with eleven girls and eleven boys. Seven of these children come from non-English speaking backgrounds.

My approach to teaching is based on whole language principles where language is integrated across the curriculum. Emphasis is placed on interactive oral language activities in all areas.

How a Spelling Journal is Used in my Class

Approximately half-way through the year, I gave journals to those children who demonstrated advanced language skills (i.e. on the spelling and writing continua). By the end of Term Three all children were using journals.

- Initially, children identified key words (i.e. words important to them—family names, pet names, theme words, etc.). I printed two words per day into their journals and the children self-tested at home.
- After the children had completed four parent tests, the fifth test was with me. I usually find time to work on the spelling journals during daily writing sessions.
- Once the children can spell their two words they select another two. Most children continue to practise two words daily but some have increased this to five words.
- Midway through Term Three the more advanced writers and spellers began proof reading and editing some of their own writing. They circle any words in their writing which they consider should be included in their journal.
- Approximately once every month I, or my aide, individually test ten words from each child's list of journal words. This written test is pasted into their work sample folder and sent home.
- When scoring written tests I give a score for correct words as well as the total number of correct letters.
- 'Have-a-go' folders were introduced in the last two weeks of Term Three. Words are sometimes selected from this source for home practice.

How the Journals Assist Evaluation of Spelling Development

- by monitoring each child's selection of words (some children choose 'safe' words, others enjoy the challenge of difficult words)
- by having regular teacher-tests after parent testing (these tests are conducted informally—children like printing their words on the chalk-board)
- by having the monthly review test of ten words
- *most importantly, observing the transfer of correct spelling to children's writing*
- I also place children on the *Spelling Developmental Continuum* twice a year.

Conclusions

(A) Children

- The children all appear to enjoy the challenge of learning and using their personal words. Interest level is high and there appears to be a great sense of accomplishment.
- The children seem much more prepared to 'have-a-go' when writing and try more difficult words.
- The use of personal spelling journals really encourages children and extends their spelling awareness.

(B) Teacher

- Introduction and use of spelling journals initially requires considerable teacher direction. It can be time consuming until the children understand the process and can work effectively with peers.
- Parents appreciate the regular home practice.
- The use of spelling journals has broadened my appreciation of what children can do when given control of their own learning. Motivated children develop a spelling ability far beyond the prescribed lists once taught in classrooms.

Example 2

Teacher: Jenny Snell

Class: Year 1/2 (five, six and seven year olds)

Using Spelling Journals in a Year 1/2 Classroom

The spelling journal was started with a group of twelve, Year 2 children early in the year.

The main reason for adopting this approach, as opposed to using spelling lists was based on several observations:

- the children were already capable spellers, having had a very good grounding in year one;
- the year two spelling lists as set out in *My Word Book* seemed irrelevant and inappropriate and the thought of teaching from it made me feel quite uninspired; and
- I believe spelling is for writing, therefore lists are irrelevant (although the Salisbury List was used as a starting point).

How a Spelling Journal is Used in my Class

It took the best part of term one to introduce the format to the students. This problem was compounded by the fact that I teach only three days a week and the children did not get sufficient follow through. This did not deter me however. A further delay was the fact that I had to make my own journals although I was able to modify several ideas to create a working journal. I have to admit that there were days when I wondered whether I was too ambitious, however by the end of the term I could see the beginnings of some very pleasing work.

We started slowly and for several weeks I had to repeat the process at the start of each lesson.

The organisation was as follows:

1 The children wrote down a selection of words from the 'have-a-go' pad. I encouraged their own decisions as to the number of words. Some chose five, others as many as ten. These words were written onto pre-cut card and placed into the word bank.

2 The children spent the remainder of the lesson learning the words following the LOOK, SAY, COVER, WRITE, CHECK method. Scrap pads were provided.

3 When they felt they were ready, the students formed partnerships with others in their group and then tested each other on their words.

4 Any words that were correct were placed into the next box. Mistakes were placed back into the previous box.

5 This procedure was continued until all words were placed into the teacher test box.

6 When there were approximately 15-20 words in the teacher box, a teacher test was given.

7 After the teacher test, all words that were correctly spelt were written on the page titled *Words I Now Know*.

8 These words then became the basis of term tests. If the pupil had not been able to maintain his or her spelling knowledge of these words they then went back into the journal.

How the Journal Assists Evaluation of Spelling Development

1 Children work at their individual level whilst being challenged.

2 Children can work at their own pace without being held back by slower pupils or the constraints of a spelling list.

3 The words that the pupils learn are relevant to the individual's writing style, ability and interest.

4 Pupils learn their words thoroughly because of the repetitive nature of the program without suffering the boredom of list words. The students themselves thought they learned the words better.

5 Use of peer assistance fosters a positive learning environment. The pupils are involved in each other's achievements and praise each other accordingly.

6 Some students actually like the partner test!

7 Children are not compared with each other, therefore the weaker students still have the opportunity to achieve high scores.

8 Suits all ability levels.

Points to consider:

- Start slowly.
- Check that the children copy words correctly.
- Children still make a lot of errors in their writing and some errors may be overlooked. It is important to monitor this and have children copy these words into spelling journal on the page titled *Words I Need to Know*.
- Some children who are very poor spellers in their writing may be daunted by the sheer numbers of words they need to learn. They need lots of encouragement.

  PERSEVERE! IT IS WORTH IT!

Conclusions

In concluding I would like to add that I became very curious as to how these students would rate on a St Lucia spelling test. I had felt for some time that they had gone beyond the journal. These children were so competent that I considered they needed extension in other language or spelling areas. I administered the test and found that they had spelling ages between 11.0 and 13.5. These were the students that I would find pouring over dictionaries and atlases looking for words to spell!

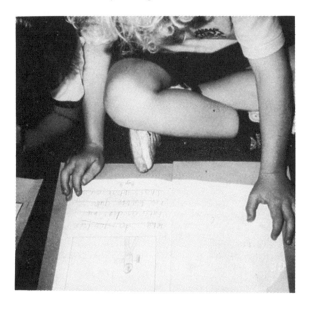

Spelling Journal
Year 2

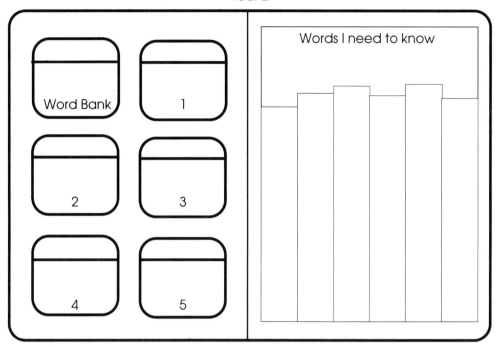

'Have-a-go' Pad

sh	ae	i-e	o-e	ee	oo	i r	str	scr	squ
ch	ai	igh	ow	ea	ew	er	thr	spr	spl
wh	ay	y	oa	u	ue	ur	or	old	dge
th	ar	ie	Silent letter h	ie	u	ear	all	o	age
ng	a	oi	k	h	w	air	aw	ear	ind
qu	ae	oy	h	l	t	ear	au	wor	alk
tch	ice	wg	n	g	u	are	are	war	
ph	d ce	ea	ow	ou	oo	u	oar		

My Column	Teacher's Column	My Column	Teacher's Column

Test Pad

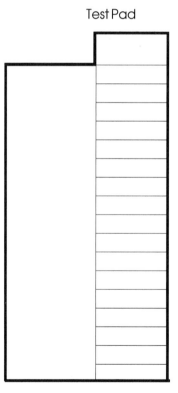

Example 2—formats of spelling journal materials

Example 3

Teacher: Judy Hayden

Class: Year 3 (seven and eight year olds)

Using Spelling Journals in a Year 3 Classroom

My Year 3 class consists of twelve boys and twelve girls. Five children come from non-English speaking families where either no English is spoken at all, very little is spoken or only one parent speaks English. One child is part-Aboriginal.

I have been using a whole language approach based on themes with the children and I have been integrating language across the curriculum.

Spelling is timetabled for a thirty minute session daily although I never fail to use any opportunity that arises for incidental teaching.

Purpose

The purpose of the journal in my classroom is to enhance the spelling awareness of all the children and to help the children learn to spell correctly the words they most frequently use in their own writing.

How a Spelling Journal is Used in my Class

The journal I have been using is a modification of the First Steps journal. I only use one page with a 'Words To Learn' column, a 'Key features' column and five testing columns and a transfer column. The pages are photocopied and stapled together with an attractive and appropriate cover.

The children's errors on the Salisbury word list become their first words to be learnt. Depending on the child's ability, each child has between seven and ten words to learn at any one time. The children who had many errors continued until all the words were learnt. The children with no errors were asked for ten words they wanted to learn to spell correctly. The children with a few errors supplemented their list with words of their own choosing.

Subsequent lists of words are provided from two sources. One is the children's own 'have-a-go' pad and the other is a chart of words based on the current topic or theme which has been brainstormed by the children. The children choose any words from this list that they can't spell but wish to be able to spell.

I have also developed a set of activity cards. These cards outline the activity the child has to do on his own set of words for that day. Each card covers 'look, cover, write, check', partner testing and recording. It also provides two or three other activities for the children to do. They may have to give synonyms or antonyms for their words, circle special sounds or put their hardest word into a sentence and so on. Cards are numbered and rotated daily.

Format for Use

Each list of ten words is worked on for a two week period as follows:

Day 1   –   Cross off words that have been learnt. Transfer words not learnt to the new list. Add new words chosen from 'Have-a-go' pad or Teacher's list. Complete key features. Do, 'look, cover, write, check'.

Day 2   –   Look, cover, write, check. Partner testing and recording. Activity cards.

Day 3   –   as for Day 2.

Day 4   –   Teaching a spelling rule.

Day 5 – Look, cover, write, check, partner testing and recording and activity cards.

Day 6 – Revise the spelling rule

Day 7 – Look, cover, write check, partner testing and recording. Activity cards.

Day 8 – Crossword puzzle or word sleuth.

Day 9 – Spelling games—What Comes Next, Hang The Man, etc. Teacher test.

Day 10 – Revision exercises for weaker children. Extension activities for bright children, e.g. make up own word sleuth on their list of words.

The children do five tests with their partners. Words with at least three consecutive ticks preferably in the last three tests are considered to be learnt and can be crossed off.

Each child has a small pad—one side is for look, cover, write, check and the other is for partner testing. After the children have tested each other and marked their own words, they must bring their pad to me each time for checking before recording their result.

At the end of each fortnight I choose approximately half the class for individual teacher testing. I choose five of each child's words that they have crossed off as being known. This test is done on loose paper and is put into the child's sample work folder. At the end of the next fortnight I test the remaining half of the class.

The children make frequent use of the 'Have-a-go' pads. Each page has four columns. The children have three attempts themselves at spelling an unknown word and then bring their pad to me. Any correct attempt is ticked and praised. If no attempts are correct, I write the correct spelling in the fourth column. The children are also encouraged to use their 'Have-a-go' pad as a spelling resource.

How a Journal Assists the Evaluation of Spelling Development

In my experience the journal assists the bright children in learning to spell more challenging words. They don't become bored practising words they are already able to spell correctly.

Regular testing ensures that the children can in fact spell the words they have learnt. It also informs the principal and the parents of the progress being made.

It also aids the children in transferring correct spelling from their lists to their writing.

Conclusions

Using the spelling journal has finally laid to rest the fears I have held for many years that children who are bright or have a natural ability to spell are bored to tears with spelling lists. I feel now that by using the spelling journal strategy I am providing a more meaningful learning program for these children.

It also enables the weaker children to learn to spell words which are meaningful to them and does not involve them in a cycle of constant failure by having to compete with other more successful spellers.

Use of a spelling journal seems to create a spelling consciousness within the children and there is more likelihood of them transferring correct spelling from their journal into their writing.

Finally, through using a spelling journal, I feel that I am providing a more stimulating and child centred approach to the learning of spelling than I have at any previous time. **29**

Example 4

Teacher: Annette Edwards-Parker

Class: Year 4 (eight and nine year olds)

Using Spelling Journals in a Year 4 Classroom

I had a straight Year 4 class of sixteen boys and thirteen girls. Four of the children attend Education Support classes and two of this group of children are classed as Core Education Support.

Purpose of Journals in my Class

- To incorporate spelling into the total language program of the classroom
- To allow children to work on an individual program suited to their level of development
- To encourage children to take responsibility for their own spelling performance

How a Spelling Journal is Used in my Class

During the first term of the school year the classroom spelling program involved placing the children on the *Spelling: Developmental Continuum*, introducing the 'have-a-go' pad and teaching all children a bank of spelling activities that could be completed independently in the following terms. These activities were taken from the *Spelling: Developmental Continuum* Book and were chosen according to the degree of independence required to complete them and their applicability to several of the developmental phases. These activities were to later form the basis of the 'independent activities' sheet of the spelling journal (see page 32).

At the beginning of Term 2 the spelling journal was introduced into the classroom. A period of a fortnight was allowed for children to enter and study 6 to 12 words from their journals. Over the fortnight the children completed the look, cover, write, check strategy six times with each word and they also completed an 'Independent Activity sheet'. (Initially all children entered 10 words into the *class words list* and completed the same 'Independent Activity Sheet'.)

Following this initial introductory fortnight the children entered words into the *personal word list* page of their journal from two sources: their 'have-a-go' pads and from errors in their writing that had been identified by themselves/parent/teacher.

At the beginning of each fortnight 6 to 12 words were highlighted from the *personal words list* and if necessary the *class words list* depending on the child's level of ability. Each child then throughout the fortnight completed the look, cover, write, check strategy with each word and an 'Independent Activity Sheet', appropriate to their phase of development and based on their current highlighted words.

The 'Independent Activity Sheet' was changed approximately half way through each term to ensure children completed a variety of activities and were working at a level appropriate to their phase of development.

On the last Friday of the designated fortnight children 'partner-tested' their current words and recorded their results in the test columns on the *personal words list* and *class words list* sheets.

How a Spelling Journal Assists Evaluation of Spelling Development

- Observation of each child's bank of known words.
- Observation of the child transferring words correctly to their journal.
- Monitoring of each child's selection of words.
- Monitoring of independent work.

Conclusions

(A) Children

- All children are able to successfully master personal words which are useful to them in their writing.
- Children take greater responsibility for spelling performance.
- A strategy for learning new words is clearly established and supported to minimise antagonism with parents when children take the journal home to prepare for the 'partner-test.'

(B) Teacher

- Initially a great deal of direction and organisation is required by the teacher to ensure that use of journals operates smoothly. (Even to the degree of instructing children on where to complete independent activities.)
- Use of a journal allows the teacher to deal more effectively with the wide range of abilities in a class.
- Parents are reassured as they are able to use the journal to monitor their child's development.

Spelling Journal

Class Words to Learn	Independent Journal Activities	Personal Words to Learn	Personal Words to Learn
test 1 test 2 test 3 test 4	**Crossword** Create a crossword using your current words **Spelling rhymes** Create a spelling rhyme for one of your words **Cloze** Write a draft paragraph using your current words **Word Relations** Find 6 relatives of each of your current words **Synonyms** Find a synonym for each of your current words	test 1 test 2 test 3 test 4	1 2 3 4 5 6

CROSSWORD
Create a crossword using current words,
using word meanings as clues.

SPELLING RHYMES
Create a spelling rhyme for one of your
words.

CLOZE
Write a draft paragraph using your current
words, rewrite deleting these words.

WORD RELATIONS
Find 6 relatives of each of your current
words.

SYNONYMS
Find a synonym for each of your current
words.

SMALL WORDS
Find all the small words you can inside your
current words.

WORD SEARCH
Find your current words in an old magazine/
newspaper.

SPELLING RHYMES (MNEMONICS)
Create a spelling rhyme for one of your
current words.

LETTER CARDS
Construct your current words using the
letter cards.

WHO AM I?
Create a 'Who Am I?' for one of your
current words.

Examples of Independent Activity Sheets
(see page 30)

Example 5

Teacher: Heather Jolly

Class: Year 4/5 (eight, nine and ten year olds)

Using Spelling Journals in a Year 4 Classroom

The following example relates to a Year 4/5 composite class with a wide range of ability. The organisational model I have described can be adopted for Years 4-7.

Purpose of Journals in my Class

- To individualise spelling on the basis of students' writing errors. Through using a journal I am more able to meet the needs of individual children in my class.
- The journal is an excellent strategy as it is designed to enable teachers and students to work together giving the teacher the central role.
- The journal is available at all times as a resource and individual word bank.
- By monitoring students' writing across all subject areas, the teacher is able to select words for discussion, teaching and study.
- As students develop a spelling conscience and take responsibility for their learning, they are more able to analyse their own misspellings and those of their peers.

How a Spelling Journal is Used in my Class

10 mins – Teaching part of lesson

10 mins – Partner testing. Teacher corrects.
Children tick or cross results in Spelling book.

10 mins – Discuss and mark activities.
Complete activities if not finished.

Time is allowed for recording of individual words.

Children use cards for recording words from notebooks.

A 'have-a-go' pad is used for individual words.

The children have three attempts. The teacher ticks the word if it is correct. If the word is incorrect the teacher writes the word correctly in green biro and puts J after the word if it is to go into the child's journal, e.g.

Have-a-Go Pad

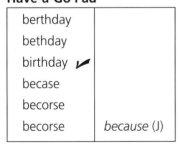

berthday	
bethday	
birthday ✓	
becase	
becorse	
becorse	*because* (J)

Italics represents teacher's entry.

Individual Student Cards

Name:_____		
health Australia magic		

The teacher records words children need for their personal writing on cards. These cards are kept in alphabetical order in a box. When going through any of the student's written work the teacher enters any words to be added to their journal on individual cards. Children add any words that have been corrected from their 'have-a-go' pads.

It is important not to overload children. Children add words from their cards into journals at a set time each week. The teacher has a record of words on cards if the student leaves their journal home on test day. (If school has fortnightly tests.)

Fortnightly Plan

Materials:
'Have-a-go' Pad, Test pad, journal, Small 'in' and 'out' trays.

Monday Day 1
Give children a topic list made up from words already discussed in Social Studies, Science, Health, Maths, Reading, Literature, etc. These are words children will want to use in their projects and writing, 15–20 words.

- The children print the topic list words in pencil into the appropriate section of their spelling journal.

The page is set out as in the diagram below

Words	Key Features (word building)	Test Records		
Australia	Australian, Australians			
ocean	oceans			
world	worlds			
write	wri<u>tt</u>en, writing			
wrote				

- Words are presented one at a time in context. There is only brief discussion as words have already been discussed in other lessons.
- When children finish printing their lists from the blackboard, they change books and their partners check to see that words are correct. The teacher *also* needs to check to see if the spelling is correct. (Children leave their books open on their desks for the teacher to quickly check).
- Spelling words are put on a sheet for homework, e.g. Tuesday's words, Wednesday's words etc. Throughout the week children learn their spelling for homework—5 words per day (look, cover, write, check).

Tuesday Day 2

- Introduce the class activity. This could be word building, or an activity that focuses on syllables, antonyms, plurals or proofing.
- Children are instructed to complete the set exercises in Spellit (or another resource) at their year level or ability level, after testing.
- Partner Testing
- (a) Children test each other in pairs (5 words from topic lists).
  (b) As test is completed, it is brought to the teacher and placed in the *in* tray.
  (c) Teacher marks these and places them in the *out* tray.
  (d) As children come out with their tests they collect those already marked and return them to their owners.
  (e) When test is returned, the child checks and records.
- Children go on with the exercises. Teacher marks exercises with the children.

Wednesday Day 3 ⎫
Thursday Day 4 ⎬ As for Day 2
Friday Day 5 ⎭

Second Week
Monday Day 6

- (a) Children work on personal lists. Each child spends ten minutes learning personal list words. (Look, cover, write, check). Words are taken from their 'have-a-go' pads. (Children have already entered words at a set time the week before.)
- (b) Children partner test personal lists as they did for topic lists. When each child finishes, they record their errors and put words in sentences.

Tuesday Day 7

- Class spelling activity. Children test five individual words and then complete set exercises.

Wednesday Day 8

- Class spelling activity. Children test five individual words and then complete set activity.

Thursday Day 9

- Children take their journals home to revise individual lists. Children complete exercises.

Friday Day 10

- Teacher supervises children testing their partner on eight individual words and then takes over and tests twelve more topic lists words with some word building words.

Marking will take the form of:

- child marking
- child marking with teacher
- teacher marking (checking results of 'partner-testing')
- teacher marking (exercises, activity work, written work after child editing)

How the Journals Assist Evaluation of Spelling Development

Information can be gathered about:

– the kinds of words children are attempting
– particular strategies the child is using when attempting words, i.e. phonetic, visual, meaning based
– acquisition of a high frequency vocabulary
– ability to identify troublesome words from personal writing
– development of proof reading skills
– application of generalisations

Conclusions

With thorough organisation and modelling, use of a spelling journal is an excellent strategy for improving students' spelling skills and understandings. I have found that a result of this approach is increased risk taking by children and an improved attitude towards spelling.

Example 6

Teacher: Paul Stein

Class: Year 6 (ten and eleven year olds)

Using Spelling Journals in a Year 6 Classroom
Composition of Class

My class was made up of children who were all from a Non-English Speaking background. There was a dominance of children who had been in Australia less than two years. The main countries of origin were Vietnam, Indonesia and Eastern Europe.

How the Journal Approach was Implemented

1 The children used 'top-up' pads for words they found of interest in Literature, Science, Social Studies, Reading and from their own writing. Some children wrote these directly into their journal and by-passed the 'top-up' pad.
2 Pupils broke words into syllables and wrote word meanings in their journals. Others put words into sentences. If it was discovered they didn't know what a word meant they were directed to check the meaning in a dictionary.
3 Working in pairs children tested each other for the first five minutes each day. They tested the first five words and once any of these were correct (3 ticks in a row) the word was crossed off and a new one added from the children's 'top-up' pads.'
4 The five words were brought to the teacher who marked them and discussed word meanings with the children.

Where Did the Words Come From?

The words came from various sources. Children would often write words in their pads or journals during or following shared book, literature, television broadcasts, Social Studies, Science activities and many other curriculum areas.

NESB children showed increasing confidence with sound patterns. They applied words and vocabulary that was of significance and relevance to them.

'Top-up' pads—These pads are kept on the children's desks so words can be added throughout the day. The children copy the words into the 'Words to Learn' section of their journals at a set time each day.

How the Journal Assists Evaluation of Spelling Development

Over a period of time it became clear that the children's vocabulary had improved and their knowledge of word structure had increased. They seemed to become more adept at applying morphological structures and spelling patterns. Children became less inhibited with words and this reflected in all facets of language work. They were more willing to 'have-a-go', showed initiative and became quite independent with spelling.

Conclusions

The 'Spelling Journal' approach provided a valuable alternative to what I had been doing with this subject area in previous years. There was obvious improvement in the children's oral language, spelling and listening skills. It was great to see the children taking on the responsibility for learning their own spelling. The journal approach was used in conjunction with other First Steps procedures.

Example 7

Teacher: Chris Leed

Class: Year 7 (eleven and twelve year olds)

Using Spelling Journals in a Year 7 Classroom

I have a Year 7 class with thirty-one students.

The students range in ability from phonetic through to independent spellers.

I use a spelling journal with all students in my class. It provides an individualised method of treating spelling. The children are motivated by the fact that *they* are taking responsibility for learning words *they* need to know how to spell.

How a Spelling Journal is Used in my Class

Spelling Journal

Misspellings from the child's own writing are entered on the *Words to Learn* sheets. Also included are the *Subject-Specific* and *Class-Focus* words (i.e. any theme you may have running).

Testing Process

1 Each child learns five (5) words from their list each day.
2 LOOK, COVER, WRITE, CHECK. (One word at a time.)
3 Partners test each other.
4 Test pads are placed on the teacher's desk to be marked. Those already marked are returned by the student on his/her way back to desk.
5 On receiving the marked test pads, the children insert a tick or cross in the vacant column on the right side of the sheet.
6 If three consecutive ticks are gained, the words are deemed to have been effectively learned and are deleted from the list.
7 If three ticks are not gained after the child has been tested five times, a 'T' is inserted in the column; the word is deleted and re-inserted at the bottom of the list.

Analysis and Formal Instruction

When monthly error counts are completed, an analysis of error types is made and collated on a class Error Analysis sheet, using the following classifications:

- Word Study
- Phonic-vowel sounds
- Phonic-consonant sounds
- Compounding
- Affixes
- Contractions
- Homophones and homographs

Evaluation

1 Error count on a selected piece of unproofed writing. 100 words are counted and errors noted. Result is expressed as a percentage error count. This is carried out on a four weekly basis.
2 Monthly test—20 mastered words could be tested.

Sample Spelling Session

1 Discuss the day's activity. Give any necessary directions, e.g. 'Today we are looking at contractions page ...'
2 Direct children to begin self-testing. Approximately 3-4 minutes.
3 Children 'partner-test' using the strategy:
   - Say the word.
   - Say the word in a sentence. (Important if the word is a homophone.)
   - Say the word again.
4 Teacher marks the test books.
5 Children enter the results.
6 Begin the day's activity while the teacher marks the remaining books.

How the Journals Assist Evaluation of Spelling Development

Each month a selection of mastered words from the spelling journal may be tested, e.g. children can be asked to 'partner-test' each other on every second and fourth word that has been crossed off on their lists.

Conclusions

I have now used a spelling journal for six years in both middle and upper primary classes. I have used it with children of well below class average ability and those working at an independent level. In all instances I have found the children to be motivated, effective users of a journal.

I believe a 'journal approach' works in well with the concept of 'Whole Language' and ties in nicely with use of the *Spelling: Developmental Continuum*.

Chapter 3:

Teaching Graphophonics

Introduction

In recent years, there has been some discussion about whether or not graphophonics should be taught in the early years of schooling. It is known that there is a link between children's knowledge of graphophonics and their reading ability, therefore the question is not *whether* we should teach graphophonics, but *how* we should teach it. It is important that the teaching of graphophonics takes place in a context that makes sense to children, as children frequently fail to make the connection between graphophonic knowledge and reading. The problem-solving approach described in this chapter has proved to be successful with many children, particularly those who are having difficulty with reading and writing.

Phonology and Graphophonics

phonology *n.* study of sounds in a language; hence **phonological** *a.* [f. Gk *phone* voice, sound]

graph *n.*, visual symbol, esp. letter(s), representing phoneme or other feature of speech [f. Gk *graphe* writing]

Beliefs

This chapter is based on the beliefs:

- that learning about the graphophonic aspects of language plays a crucial part in developing children's reading and writing ability
- that a problem-solving approach to teaching phonics is far more powerful than teaching 'letter' stories and drilling 'sounds' because it teaches children strategies that they can use as independent learners
- that understanding graphophonics is a crucial component of word attack skills. It is important for children to learn about the symbol-sound relationships of language. There is a strong correlation between children's knowledge of graphophonic relationships and their ability to deal with words and solve problems independently when reading and writing

Principles

This chapter is based on the premise that children learn best about the relationship between sounds and symbols when:

P • They are given the opportunity to **problem-solve** these relationships for themselves through problem solving activities that call for them to work out corrections and relationships for themselves.

40

E • the problem solving is **embedded** in a context which makes sense to them. This could be from daily news sentences, familiar books, shared book activities, puzzles and strategies that call for children to think out solutions. They need to build on their existing knowledge of letters and letter names.

W • the activities and strategies in which they are involved take into account the child's **working memory**. Working memory is the number of different things a child can deal with at any one time. Children need to internalise the links between graphophonics, reading and writing so that the different pieces of the jigsaw become one big picture.

I • they are encouraged to talk while problem-solving (**interaction**). Children also need to tell others about their achievements.

T • they are given **time** to practise as they progress. The **time** needed to internalise new learning will vary from child to child

By using a problem-solving approach to discovering symbol-sound relationships in a context that makes sense to them, children will learn **processes** that will enable them to analyse and monitor language as they develop more sophisticated language skills. This approach will also help them to develop a lively curiosity about how language works.

R • when children are engaged in problem solving activities and are continually constructing new knowledge, it is crucial that they are given time and opportunities for **Reflection**

R • after children have reflected on what they have learned, it is crucial that they are able to **Represent** their knowledge in some concrete way

R • it is also extremely important that children can **Report** on what they have learned to each other and to the teacher. Explaining a concept to someone else helps to clarify and consolidate it.

Teachers Need to be Aware that:

- Young children are familiar with the sounds of spoken language, but need to develop their understandings of the written language. As they develop these understandings, they map their knowledge of phonology onto graphic symbols.
- Young children are often unable to hear individual sounds in words. Teachers may sound out a word into separate phonemes, but need to be aware that young children may not hear these as separate sounds.
- Young children can easily discriminate speech sounds when the sounds are presented in a context that makes sense to them. For example, if a teacher asked a child to discriminate between the different sounds in *bat* and *cat,* the child may not be able to segment the words by sounding out the 'b' and the 'c'. However, if a teacher said 'bat' and 'cat' and asked a child to point to the correct picture of either a bat or a cat, the child would have no difficulty.
- Children for whom English is a second language may not be able to distinguish or differentiate between the different sounds of English. Such children may subsume the sounds they hear into the familiar sounds of their own language. It is important when teaching these children to focus on visual rather than auditory patterns.

What Do Children Need to Know?

An understanding of some fundamental concepts will help young children puzzle out symbol-sound relationships and generalise from what they learn.

Children need to know:

- letter names, not sounds, when they first begin to ask about letters, because
    letter names are constant, whereas sounds vary
    children use letter names to invent spelling and thus begin to puzzle out how to write words
- that letters often represent different sounds. For example, with a child named Anne, 'This is the letter 'A' and in your name, it says 'a' like ant', or with a child named Amy, 'In your name, it says 'a' like ate'
- That letters sometimes work alone and sometimes in groups; for example, *me, bread, sheet, team*
- That the sound a letter or group of letters represents depends on where the letter is in a word and what other letters surround it; for example, *cat, city, Christmas, chop*
- That the same sound can be represented by different letters; for example, *beach, me, key, ski, thief*
- That the same letters may represent different sounds; for example, *rough, cough, dough, plough*

Teachers need to be aware that the symbol-sound relationships that children discover will not follow a neat pattern and are best post-programmed. Children will learn more quickly and more soundly if they focus on elements which have current meaning for them, rather than the teacher. If teachers see a need to treat a symbol that children have not focused on, the context can be manipulated to ensure the symbol occurs.

It is important that children understand from the beginning that one letter may represent a range of sounds. They will gradually discover what these sounds are as they extend their experience of the written language over time.

What Might Children Already Know?

Young children who have had many opportunities to play with, explore and puzzle out the written language will gradually be developing:

- understandings of the concepts of print:
    speech can be written down
    the message is in the print
    print is constant
    a word can be separated from the object or idea it represents
    numbers and letters are different
- understandings of the conventions of print:
    print goes left to right
    print goes top to bottom
    a word is a unit of print with space on either side
    what a page is
    what a book is
- their own logical, rule-based knowledge of symbol-sound relationship. For example, one child began a letter, 'Dear evreebodee.' Another child wrote 'Bh' for *beach* because she could hear 'ch' in 'aitch.' The rules children develop may not be accurate in terms of conventional spelling but they are invariably logical in child terms.

- early understandings about spelling often relying on letter names. For example:
  Mi — my; Kv — cave; Lrfnt — elephant; Cr — car; Sosij — sausage; Cd — seed;
  Ppl —people.
  For further elaboration on this see the *Spelling: Developmental Continuum*.
- the ability to puzzle out print and make connections. This is illustrated by the
  following sample of writing. The child is puzzling out how to spell 'Mothers' Day.'
  By the end of the piece, the child came close to the conventional spelling.

An Effective Way of Teaching Phonics

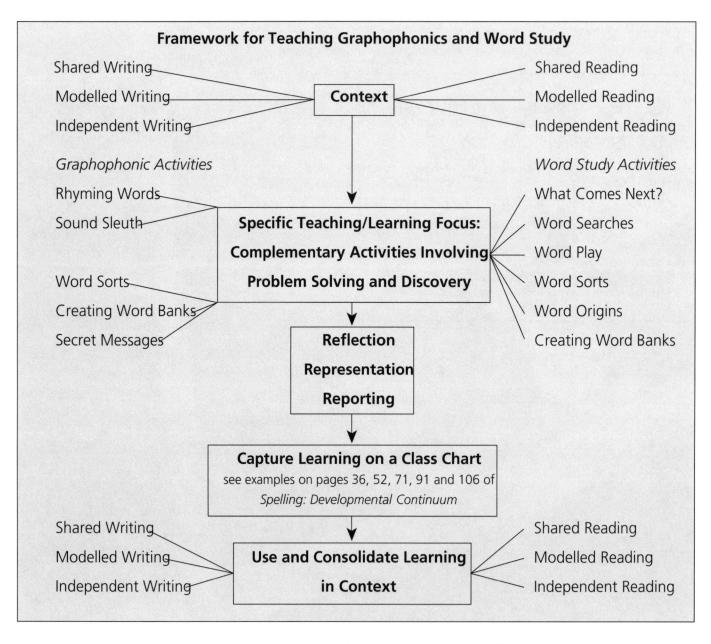

Framework for Teaching Graphophonics and Word Study

Shared Writing
Modelled Writing — **Context**
Independent Writing

Shared Reading
Modelled Reading
Independent Reading

Graphophonic Activities

Rhyming Words
Sound Sleuth

Word Sorts
Creating Word Banks
Secret Messages

Specific Teaching/Learning Focus:
Complementary Activities Involving
Problem Solving and Discovery

Word Study Activities

What Comes Next?
Word Searches
Word Play
Word Sorts
Word Origins
Creating Word Banks

Reflection
Representation
Reporting

Capture Learning on a Class Chart
see examples on pages 36, 52, 71, 91 and 106 of
Spelling: Developmental Continuum

Shared Writing
Modelled Writing
Independent Writing

Use and Consolidate Learning
in Context

Shared Reading
Modelled Reading
Independent Reading

Because the written language is concrete and offers visual patterns, it makes sense for learners to begin with symbols instead of sounds. Some children, particularly Aboriginal children, tend to be visual learners and benefit from this approach.

Note: Teachers who work with ESL children should not focus on sounds, because these children cannot hear the differences in sounds; but should encourage children to work from visual patterns.

In the Preliminary Phase, this means:

- that children need to be given many opportunities to 'write' and 'read', if they choose to, in situations that relate to the real world. Examples are: recipes in the 'kitchen'; prescriptions in the 'doctor's surgery'; lists; notices and signs in the 'shop'
- that children need to be made aware that adults read and write for a variety of purposes
- that children need to be surrounded by print that they have had some part in composing, e.g.

  poems
  lists of songs they know
  language experience sentences
  books on their maths activities
  writing under their class murals

- that children sometimes need to have their attention drawn to letters, words, sentences, patterns and so on, during activities such as shared reading and modelled writing
- that children need to build on their awareness of environmental print

In the Semi-phonetic Phase and beyond, this means:

- that children need to have opportunities to puzzle out symbol-sound relationships
- that teachers need to present children with activities that require them to problem-solve in a context that makes sense to them
- that teachers need to be aware that the symbol-sound relationships that children discover will not follow a neat pattern and are best post-programmed. If teachers see a need to treat a symbol that children have not focused on, the context can be manipulated to ensure the symbol occurs
- that once children have focused on a particular symbol-sound relationship, teachers need to provide further activities to consolidate learning
- that charts or word banks that reinforce children's discoveries need to be displayed around the room. If a piece of paper is stuck to the base of each, children can add new words or patterns to it as they discover them, and teachers can then add their discoveries to the original chart
- that all children are catered for at their individual levels of understanding
- that some contexts that best support the problem-solving approach are:

  daily writing
  blackboard news sentences
  shared books, text innovations
  modelled writing
  weather charts
  charted songs and poems
  language experience work
  activities which call for thinking, not copying

Some Significant Activities

Sound Sleuth

This activity underpins the teaching of graphophonic relationships. Children can become 'Sound Sleuths' in any context where they are involved with meaningful print. A few of these contexts are suggested in the following section.

Suggestions are offered regarding possible focuses for teaching and learning at different phases of development. Teachers will find, however, that they are led by the children. Sometimes children will pursue an understanding far beyond the limits which an externally structured program would impose on them. On other occasions children may miss something which seems very simple, in which case the teacher will say nothing, but will ensure that they encounter the same concept again in a different context so that they are again challenged by the concept.

If children's discoveries are charted on the class chart, as suggested in the *Spelling: Developmental Continuum* book, the teacher will have a precise record of the learning which has ocurred and will be able to re-visit any gaps which are apparent.

Preliminary Phase

A major focus for teaching in the preliminary phase is placed on the sounds represented by initial letters. Before they make any connections between symbol and sound, children will make connections between the initial letter of their names and the same letter when they see it in another word, especially when the letter is written in upper case. The children's names make a good starting point for graphophonic teaching, enabling children to make connections between the initial letter and sound of their names and the same initial letter and sound when they encounter it in other well known words.

- Talk to the children about their first day of school and write one or two simple sentences on the blackboard. Break the sentences into chunks of meaning.
- Read the sentences several times and get the children to 'read' them with you.
- Ask the children if anyone knows what an 'm' looks like. Use the letter name, not the sound.
- Write M, m on the blackboard.
- Ask if anyone has a name which starts with M. Write it/them down.
- Get children to draw rings around the words with M, m in them.
- Say the words with the children and get them to listen to the sound the M, m makes.
- List all the words with M, m in them.
- Ask the children to hunt for more M, m words to add to the list.
- Go through the list at the end of the day and ask the children to see if M, m always makes the same sound.
- Chart the most interesting M, m words and draw pictures next to them so the children can 'read' them.
- Stick a piece of paper to the bottom of the chart for adding new words.

Semi-Phonetic Phase

In the Semi-Phonetic phase children are encouraged to investigate the range of sounds represented by a single letter. Again, a good starting point is a name, e.g.

Carol, Charles, Celeste. Praise children for their discoveries and place them on the class chart. Give children time and be prepared to wait for them to extend their understandings as they continue to collect evidence. They will not find out everything at once, but will gradually work out extensions of rules as they are confronted by a new challenge, e.g. that 'c' sometimes sounds like 's'. In this phase children will focus on the most obvious sound in a word. Children will also become increasingly aware of vowel sounds and will often connect these with names of the vowels.

Phonetic Phase and Beyond

In the Phonetic phase children explore different ways of representing the same sounds, e.g. door, saw, more. A major focus is placed on medial vowel sounds and children find that breaking words into syllables helps them to work out the sounds of words effectively.

A recount, report or other text-type can be written on the blackboard or in butcher's paper in a shared writing session. Children can be challenged to list words according to letter patterns which represent a specific sound, e.g. E as in 'been'. The words containing this sound can be written on the class chart, having been classified according to the letter pattern. A piece of paper can be appended to the chart so that children can add more words as they come across them during their daily work.

Rhyming Words

Preliminary phase

Some children in the preliminary phase may not yet have developed the ability to recognise rhyme and may need a great deal of practice and adult support to help them understand the concept. Teachers may sometimes think that children can recognise rhyming words because they are able to sort cards with words and pictures on them into pairs, however, it may be that children have learned to use other strategies such as memory or letter pattern cues to accomplish the task. The ability to recognise rhyme emerges before the ability to generate ryhmes.

Rhyming Words Card Game
- Select pairs of rhyming words which are familiar to the children and can be easily illustrated, e.g. cat/mat, dog/frog, pig/dig, bun/run.
- Make a pack of cards with one word and a picture on each card. Familiarise the children with the words and pictures before they are used in a game. Two or three children play with the teacher or another adult.
- Cards are shuffled and dealt out.
- Players look at their cards and see if they have any rhyming pairs. If they have these are placed on the table and named—'I've got star and car'. The adult will need to help children identify the pairs. Encourage children to talk about the words.
- The first player asks the player on his/her left 'Have you got a word which rhymes with (cat)?' The adult can help a child make a decision saying 'Does cat sound the same as pig—cat/pig? Does cat sound the same as run—cat/run? Does cat sound the same as mat—cat/mat?'
- If the child identifies a rhyming pair the cards are put on the table and the child has another turn. If not, the next child chooses a word card from his/her set and, with help, questions the player on his/her left.

Rhyming Names

In the preliminary phase a great deal can be done to enhance children's understanding of rhyme through playing with their names. Rhyming couplets can be devised for each child, e.g.

We are very proud of Ben
He writes so nicely with his pen

Trevor
is clever

If the name does not lend itself to rhyme, incorporate it elsewhere in the couplet,

Simon has a lovely book
I hope he lets us have a look

Sylvana likes to write and draw
Every day she does some more

Nursery Rhymes, Songs and Jingles

Familiar rhymes can be used to foster children's understanding of rhyme. Children can 'help' the teacher find alternative rhymes such as:

Jack and Pete went up the street to fetch a pail of water, or

Humpty Dumpty sat on a rock
Humpty Dumpty had a big shock, or

Round and round the garden
Like a little mouse
One step, two step
Back into the house

The children are able to focus on the rhyming word most effectively if as few of the rest of the words as possible are changed.

Semi-Phonetic Phase

Rhyming Snap

The pack of cards which was used for the Rhyming Pairs game in the Preliminary phase can be enlarged and used for playing Snap. Children can initially play with an adult until they are confident enough to play independently in pairs.

Rhyming Words
Finish these:

log   mat   road

The cat sat on the - - -
The frog jumped off the - - -
The toad hopped onto the - - - -

When children are confident, they can fill the gap without the help of the words to choose from.

Rhyming Chain

Children start with a simple one syllable word such as 'bat' and take turns to think of a rhyme. The words are written into the links of a chain on the blackboard as they are suggested.

Phonetic Phase
Rhyming Riddles

The answers to these riddles rhyme with *at*

> I have ears and a tail.
> I drink milk.
> I say meow.
> I am a - - - .

> I love eating cheese.
> I have a long tail.
> I am a - - - .

> I hit balls.
> People play cricket with me.
> I am a - - - .

The answers to these riddles rhyme with *chair*

> I live in a cave or at the zoo.
> One of my friends is called Yogi.
> I am a - - - - .

> I have four sides.
> I have four corners.
> I am a - - - - - - .

> You eat me.
> I am yellow.
> I am a fruit.
> I am a - - - - .

Are all these rhyming words spelt the same way?

How are they different?

Can you think of any more words that rhyme with these words?

Transitional Phase

Cloze and Clues

Construct cloze activities or definitions for which all answers have the same sound, such as 'oo' as in moon, blue, you, through; or the same visual pattern such as 'oo' as in spoon, flood or stood.

These words rhyme with 'you'.	These words have 'oo' in them.
Last night I saw the *(moon)* shining.	You eat your soup with this. *(spoon)*
The bird *(flew)* up to its nest.	After the cyclone there was a big *(flood)*.

How many different ways can you find to spell the sound 'oo' as in moon?

How many other words can you find with 'oo' in them?

Does the 'oo' always make the same sound?

Secret Messages

The ability to segment and blend letters and letter clusters is an important skill in decoding. The 'Secret Message' activity provides children with the opportunity to decode messages by manipulating letters and letter clusters to make new words.

- **To get started, put a secret message on the blackboard every day and work it out as a class. As children become proficient, they can begin to work independently. Remember to put the alphabet at the bottom of each message for easy access.**
- Although it is not appropriate to focus heavily on segmenting and blending until children reach the Phonetic phase, it is very helpful if the concept of secret messages is introduced in the Preliminary phase.

- Give the children 'Spy Pads' so they can work out the solutions by writing the words, crossing out bits and adding to them.
- If children are not competent readers, put a picture by the key word; for example, Take 'b' off *book* and put in 'l.'
- After modelling, older children may attempt to write their own secret messages.
- Keep copies of all activities and build a permanent collection of them.

Some examples of Secret Messages constructed to suit children at different phases of development are shown in subsequent pages.

Preliminary Phase

Write a simple message which combines words with word-pictures and help children decode it, e.g.

Sit on the mat

Children love this activity and soon learn to decode messages by themselves. Although at this phase there is no focus on letters and sounds, this activity will help children to develop their understandings about the relationship between the spoken and written language and their concept of a word.

Semi-Phonetic Phase

At this phase children can deal with secret messages which involve rhyming words and intial letter sounds, provided that support is given by the teacher. Always have the alphabet displayed where children can use it for a reference.

A variety of clues, such as those shown below, can be used; for instance initial letters(1), alphabet knowledge (2) and word knowledge (3).

A B C D E F G H I J K L M N O P Q R S T U V W X Y Z

1   Take 'B' off 'Bit' and add 'S' __ __ __
2   The letter after 'N' and the letter after 'M' __ __
3   The first word in this sentence __ __ __
4   Take 'd' off 'door' and put in 'fl'__ __ __ __ __

__ __ __   __ __   __ __ __   __ __ __ __ __.

Note

It is important when giving a clue that the new word has the same sound as the old word; for example: Take 'st' off stood and put in 'h'; **not** take 'bl' off 'blood' and put in 'h'.

Phonetic Phase

In this phase the children can decode clues independently and may focus specifically on segmenting and blending as in the examples shown below.

A B C D E F G H I J K L M N O P Q R S T U V W X Y Z

Take 'mo - - - r' off mother. __ __ __
Add 'ball' to 'foot'. __ __ __ __ __ __ __ __
Take 'h' off 'his'. __ __
Rhymes with 'pin'. __ __
Take 'fa - - - r' off 'father'. __ __ __
Rhymes with 'you' but starts with 'sh'. __ __ __ __
Rhymes with 'fox' and starts with 'b'. __ __ __

__ __ __   __ __ __ __ __ __ __ __   __ __   __ __
__ __ __   __ __ __ __ __ __ __ __.

A B C D E F G H I J K L M N O P Q R S T U V W X Y Z
Take 'b' off 'book' and put in 'l'. __ __ __ __
Take 'p' off 'pin'. __ __
Take 'cr' off 'cry' and put in 'm'. __ __
Take 'fl' off 'flag' and put in 'b'. __ __ __
Take 'h' off 'hand'. __ __ __
Take 'p' off 'pet' and put in 'g'.__ __ __
Take 'fl' off 'fly' and put in 'm'. __ __
Take 'h' off 'hen' and put in 'p'. __ __ __

— — — — — — — — — — —

— — — — — — — — — — —

Transitional Phase

From this phase onwards secret messages can be used to focus on any aspect of spelling which seems to merit special attention. An example of this could be syllabification, as shown below:

1   Put the first syllable of compose before 'p' and the last syllable of delete after 'p'.
2   A one-syllable word which begins with 'y' and sounds like 'door'.
3   The first syllable is the prefix 'pro' and the second syllable of 'injection'.
4   A one-syllable word which rhymes with high and begins with 'b'.
5   The first syllable is the first three letters of fright and the second syllable is the same as the third syllable of Saturday.

— — — — — — — — — — —

— — — — — — — — — — — — — — —

Chapter 4:

Word Study and Proof Reading

Introduction

This section is based on a problem-solving approach to teaching word study skills and presents a natural sequence to the section on graphophonics. As children's understanding of graphophonics grows and expands beyond simple symbol/sound relationships, they need to extend their knowledge of word derivations, and of how words work.

By using a problem-solving based approach to word study, children will learn processes that will enable them to analyse and monitor language as they develop more sophisticated language skills. This approach will also help them to develop a lively curiosity about how language works.

Learning Objectives

Learning about words is an individual process and, to improve their skills in spelling, children need to:

- build their own lists of words and learn them
- know how to learn difficult words
- have easy access to correct spelling models
- develop an understanding of and ability to use spelling rules
- build specific-interest, subject-related and vocabulary extension lists
- be given opportunities to explore language and play with words to increase their knowledge about words
- be encouraged to discover rules and definitions for themselves through problem solving and puzzling out rules and definitions
- accept responsibility for their own learning. This includes learning how to spell correctly
- be involved in open-ended activities and be able to work at their own level of competency
- have fun when learning how language works

Children in the phonetic phase rely on the use of sound and symbol relationships to help their spelling. To help these children make further progress with their spelling, teachers need to provide experiences that will increase children's word awareness and develop their use of visual cues, knowledge of word origins, base words and word relationships.

See the chart on page 44—'Framework for Teaching Graphophonics and Word Study'.

Some Significant Activities

What Comes Next?

- This game is excellent for teaching common English letter sequences and useful for revising words from children's personal word lists. It is similar to the old game of 'Hang the Man', with the difference that the letters must be found in the correct order.
- As children guess the letters, they write the guesses that could be correct on the left as sequential letter strings, e.g. *ya/yo/yi; yet/yel/yea*. Those that could <u>not</u> be correct are written on the right. Letters on the right are written as single units such as b/f/w/m as children should not be exposed to incorrect letter patterns. A penalty is only exacted for guesses that could not be correct.
- If children take too long to guess the first letter, it may be useful to limit the number of guesses they may have, or to give them clues such as "The letter after x and before z".
- It is essential that children have access to an alphabet while playing the game.
- Discuss whether children's guesses are possible or impossible. When children guess a letter that couldn't be right, a segment of a mouse is drawn. To make the game last longer extra whiskers can be added.
  The game ends if the drawing is completed before the children guess the word.
  (An example is shown below.)

Example of 'What Comes Next?'
If the word chosen is *yesterday*, the game may look like this:

COULD BE	Y E S T __ __ __ __ __	**COULDN'T BE**
ya		i
yo		c
yet		j
yel		b

Preliminary Phase

At this phase the game can be played using **children's names**. A list of class names should be placed where all the children can see it. The teacher can initially choose a name with an initial letter which is not duplicated and then move on to one with and initial letter and then a second letter which is common to several children, such as 'S'—Simone, Sean Sally, Sandra, Sam.

Semi-Phonetic Phase

Short words can be used which are very familiar to the children. Words can be chosen which the children frequently encounter in their reading and often use in their writing, e.g. cup, cot, cat, car, cave, can; hop, he, hit, hat, had, have.
Frequently used words which children need to be able to spell without stopping to think such as the, was, mum, has should also be included.

Phonetic Phase

A strong focus can be placed on words that typify **visual patterns** and **common letter sequences**, e.g.string, witch, chief, break . The game can also be used to reinforce the understanding that a letter or letter pattern can represent more than one sound, as in zoo, blood, good and that the same sound can be represented by a range of letter patterns, as in good, wolf, put, could.

Transitional Phase

In this phase words can be chosen which represent more **complex letter patterns** which children may find difficult such as enough, attention, height, picture, bought. Simpler letter patterns such as ea, ee and ey may also need reinforcement.

Independent Phase

Latin, Greek and French derivatives can be selected, e.g. aqua (Latin-water) or atmos (Greek-vapour). **Difficult words which continue to present problems** can be dealt with in this context, e.g. cemetery, immobile, accommodate.

Word Sorts

Word Sorting and Categorising activities help children to identify visual and graphophonic relationships and patterns. They provide children with opportunities to categorise and classify words.

There are two types of word sorting activities:

Closed Sorts

The categories into which words are to be placed are given by the teacher. For example, the children may be asked to sort the words according to initial letters, common sounds or letter patterns.

Some examples of Closed Sorts:

Sort out all the words which begin with <u>dr</u>

drink	bring
didn't	drop
bike	giraffe
dress	brick
drip	grass

Sort out all the words with two syllables

flower	car
pen	ruler
glue	table
paper	sight
rubber	glass
bike	wind

Sort out the word with an <u>ai</u> sound

fly	nine	did
light	rain	my
bird	child	tie
time	bright	
mild	kick	
cry	tight	

Open Sorts

In Open Sorts no categories are given. Children study the words carefully to find their own relationships and make appropriate categories. This type of activity encourages divergent and inductive thinking.

Some examples of Open Sorts:

- A child chooses any bank of words that has been created by the class, such as an explosion chart of words relating to a specific topic, and decides what classification will be used for sorting.
- Children may choose words from their Spelling Journals
- Children may choose interesting words from books.
- Sometimes children, or the teacher, may create a word sort activity for others to carry out. The words may be presented, but the choice of category may be open, e.g.

Sort these words
Decide on your own categories.

mouse	tree	scissors	bird
elephant	lion	machine	frog
mango	monkey	flower	possum
squirrel	giraffe	mole	donkey
magpie			

- Sometimes a word sort activity may be set up which presents children with a specific problem to solve. Note that a child's solution may be quite different from that in the teacher's mind, but may still be absolutely acceptable.

Guess my rule?

mouse	cat
pig	mole
cow	dog

animals of one-syllable words

monkey	magpie
donkey	possum
mango	scissors
squirrel	

two-syllable words

mouse	mango
monkey	machine
mole	magpie

all start with 'm'

Modelling

It is important to model the process of sorting with the whole class before asking children to complete word sorts on their own or in groups.

Children can sort words related to class topics, words from class lists or class word banks.

Preliminary Phase

In this phase children can enjoy sorting activities which are not directly related to spelling. They can, for instance, sort picture cards into categories such as animals and transport. The picture cards can have the name of the animal or object printed on them, because this will foster children's developing concept of a word, but their attention will be directed towards the picture not the print. They may also enjoy sorting name cards and object cards into two piles.

When children are ready, it is a good idea to start sorting the names of some of the class. These can be carefully chosen so that two or three initial letter groups can be created. Children will sort according to the letters, not according to the sounds they represent.

56

Semi-Phonetic Phase

In this phase the main focus will be on initial letters, but if Open Sorts are encouraged children may choose to explore different categories if the words they are sorting offer viable alternatives.

An example of Closed Sorts:

initial letters

bad	cat	helicopter
bin	come	house
bat	cup	hop
black	Christine	he
boss	Christmas	happy
baby	here	
bit		
black		

An Open Sort category that might be chosen by a child could be long words and short words.

Phonetic Phase

In this phase any specific focus which needs reinforcement can be chosen. It is extremely important that children are given many opportunities to choose categories for themselves in Open Sort activities, as this encourages children to take risks and explore words for themselves.

Examples of sorts proposed by children could be:

same sound represented by different letter patterns

key
flea
see
each
ski
scheme
chief

same letter patterns representing different sounds

or

cork
worm
tractor

ear

pear
hear
pearl
heart

irregular plurals

sheep
children
men
women
mice
hooves

57

Transitional and Independent Phases

In these phases any closed sorts will be dictated by the needs of the children. Extremely creative categories will emerge during Open Sort sessions.

compound words
houseboat
bedroom
basketball
hairbrush

same letter pattern representing different sounds
bough
through
though
enough
thought

common roots
aquaduct
aquatic
aquarium

Word Sort Games

The traditional games of Tic Tac Toe, Concentration, Rummy, Snap and Fish provide an excellent context for word sorts.

Word Sort 'Tic-Tac-Toe'

- Make a game board by dividing a piece of cardboard into nine equal sections (three by three).
- One word card is placed in each section.
- Players are given eight word cards and markers.
- Children then take turns to make a category with one of their cards and one of the cards on the board using any word feature they find.
- If the children's justification is accepted the player's marker is placed on that square.
- Players continue until someone wins the game by placing three markers in a row diagonally, vertically or horizontally.

Word Sort 'Concentration'

- Shuffle a set of word cards.
- Place sixteen cards face down on the table.
- Each player in turn, turns over two cards and attempts to link the words in some way, e.g. by beginning sound, number of syllables or meaning.
- If the player can justify the link and the others accept it, the child can pick up the two cards, then turn over two more.
- If on the next try a link cannot be made, the child replaces the pair face down and another player goes through the procedure.
- The player who picks up the most cards is the winner.

Word Sort 'Rummy'

- Each player is dealt five cards and the remaining cards are placed face down in a pile. The top card is turned face up.
- The first player may take the card on the top of the face-down deck or the upturned card.
- When a player picks up a card another must be put down.
- The aim is to collect pairs of words which are linked in some way.

Word Sort 'Snap'

Snap requires the matching of particular types of information. The game can be adapted to include different types of phonetic, visual or morphemic information.

- Each player is dealt a number of snap cards face down.
- Each player in turn places one card face up.
- If that card matches the previous card in any way then the players must call out 'snap' and justify their action.
- The first player to make an acceptable connection takes all the cards which have been revealed.
- The winner is the player with the most cards at the end of the game.

Word Sort 'Guess My Group'

Each child has ten words to sort into as many categories as possible. Other children guess the criteria that have been used.

Word Origins

Knowledge of word origins helps children to:

- spell root words and related words
- decode unfamiliar words
- understand the meaning of words

Word origins are best taught in context, such as during social studies, science or mathematics.

A Suggested Teaching Strategy

- Focus on a root from Greek, Latin, French.
- Tell the children that a root is a part of a word which has its own meaning and often comes from another language such as Greek, Latin or French.
- Introduce a root such as *aqua*. Tell the children some words with that root in it and ask them to tell you the meaning of the words:

aquatic	growing or living in water
aquamarine	a bluish-green colour like water
aqueduct	artificial bridge for conveying water

- Now ask if they can deduce the meaning of *aqua*.
- Start a collection of *aqua* words on a chart or in a book. Under the chart pin a piece of paper so that children can add to the list at any time. Write the most interesting examples from the paper onto the chart.

- Display the chart at children's height so they can add cards with new words as they are discovered.

Root	Origin	Meaning	Examples
aqua	Latin	water	*aquatic, aqueduct, aquarium, aquamarine*
terra	Latin	earth	*Mediterranean, terrarium, terrestrial*
tri	Greek	three	*triangle, tripod, triathlon, triad, tricycle*

Exploring Words

(By courtesy of Judith Rivalland, Edith Cowan University)

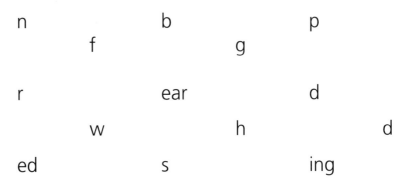

How many words can you make?

Word Searches

Listen to the children's news and blackboard a synopsis of two or three news items, leaving out the children's names, for example:

_____ brought a pet mouse to school today. It has little round eyes and long whiskers.

_____ went to Perth with his Dad. They went to see the circus.

Today it is _____ birthday. He is six years old.

- Circle known phonic patterns.
- Hunt for rhyming words, little words and big words, capital letters, silent letters.
- Ask the children who told the news. Add in the names.
- Look at a word with a new pattern or sound in it; for example, *mouse*.
- Blackboard the word and ask the children if they know any other words with that pattern or sound in them.
- Ask the children to add to this list during the day when they see other words with that pattern. Stress that this must be done in secret so as not to disturb the rest of the class.
- During the day, write the news in the class news book.
- Just before home-time, discuss the words the children have found and re-read the news.
- Provide follow-up activities during the following week.

Playing With Words

There are many activities that involve playing with and exploring language. These activities help develop a lively curiosity about language and how it works.

Crosswords

Crosswords are a fun way of playing with words. The West Ed Media computer program 'Crosswords' allows children to design their own crosswords. The Victorian Ministry of Education magazines *Comet, Explore, Challenge* and *Pursuit* have excellent crossword puzzles in them as well as other word activities on their 'Fun Pages'. Extra benefit is gained through interaction if children do crosswords with a partner or in small groups. Children can help to devise the rules for doing crosswords. Some rules could be:

- Always use pencil.
- Always print in block capitals.
- Leave the difficult clues until last.
- If a difficult answer runs down the crossword, rewrite it across the page, filling in the clues that you already have; for example, b _ o _ _.

Magic Words

Change	**H**ATE	**C**OLD	**B**IKE
	into	into	into
	LOVE	**W**ARM	**R**ACK

- The rules are:
- Change one letter at a time.
- Make a real word each time you change a letter.
- You may change the order of the letters.
- Use block letters.

As an example:

HATE	COLD	BIKE
HAVE	CORD	BAKE
HOVE	CARD	RAKE
LOVE	WARD	RACK
	WARM	

Here are some more words to change:
seas – deep, moose – roast, toes – head, walls – tiger, girl – male, wheat – bread, ship – blow.

Children's pages of newspapers and magazines often have examples of this activity.

Easier examples can be used:

	BELL	CAT
	BELT	BAT
	BOLT	BAD

Little Words in Big Words

Ask the children to see how many little words they can find in a big word; for example, **basketball.**

Rules

- You may change the order of the letters if you want.
- You may not use the same letter twice unless it is in the word twice; for example, you can make *balls* from *basketball* , but not *bases*.
- You may not use proper nouns or abbreviations; for example, you can't make *let's*, because there is no apostrophe.

Note: If there is an 's' in a word you can often make an extra word by adding an 's' and making it plural; for example, *ball, balls, bet, bets.*

When you make a little word, look carefully at it to see if you can rearrange the letters in it to make other new words before you look back at the big word again. For example, *tea, ate, eat.* Then you could make *teas* and *eats* using the *s*.

This is a good precursor for games such as Scrabble.

Word Snakes

Rules

- Find a partner.
- Get some reading material such as a basal reader, magazine, social studies book, or personal spelling list. Each person may have different material.
- Read a story, article, or extract looking for words that are nouns, verbs, adjectives, adverbs or topic-related words.
- Print a noun, verb, adjective, or adverb in the middle of a sheet of paper.
- Take turns to add a word to the end or beginning of the starter word. Each new word must use one letter of an existing word and it must change direction. Example: Word snake using nouns

Extend activity by using 1 cm squared paper and allocating points to some squares. Children can score points if letters cover the numbered squares.

Example:

	5				4	
					2	
			F³			
	5		I		2	
	3		S			
			H⁴	A	R	E¹

Fish scores   7
Hare scores   5

Square Words and Circle Words

The last letter of each word is also the first letter of the next word.

```
P E A C E
A       A
R       G
T       L
S N A K E
```

The rules are the same as for Word Snakes.

Magic Squares

This puzzle is like a crossword but the answers are the same across and down; for example:

```
B I R D
I
R
D
```

Here is an example:

1   You buy things cheaper at this.
2   Said at the end of a prayer.
3   This is in your pencil.
4   This is how the story _____.

¹S	²A	³L	⁴E
²A	M	E	N
³L	E	A	D
⁴E	N	D	S

Tic Tac Toe

Play this game exactly the same way as Noughts and Crosses, but let the children use visual patterns or sound patterns instead of the noughts and crosses.

For example, Player A may have to write words with the pattern 'ch' in them and Player B may have to use words with the letter 's' in them.

The games may look like this:

Visual Patterns: ch, s   Sounds 'i', 'e'

church	was	sorry
chemist	size	
wash	**much**	

sky	**size**	ski
bright	thief	donkey
mean		**cried**

To make the game clearer, it is useful if each child writes with a different colour.

Alliteration

Alliteration occurs when a series of words begin with the same sounds. For example, *Tania and Tony tiptoed treacherously towards the treacle tart.*
Create and discuss alternative sentences with the children.
Encourage children to generate their own sentences.
Use the sentences to illustrate an alphabet book.

Add a Letter

Start with a one-letter or two-letter word. Add one letter at a time to make a three-letter, four-letter, five-letter and six-letter word. See how far you can go. Change the order of the letters if you need to. For example:

to   not   note   tones   stones

Note: It may help some children to place words under each other if the order of the letters doesn't change.

to
tot
tote
totem

Making New Words

In this activity children are allowed to select a consonant to replace one in a particular word. The result must be a real word, e.g.

The teacher starts with
tin   pin   pit   fit   fig   rig   rip   tip

A variation focuses on the medial vowel, e.g.
tin
tan
ton

Spellamadoodle

If children need to have practice in writing a word correctly in a 'fun' way, let them construct a 'Spellamadoodle'.

1 Ask students to make a design using their spelling words printed end-to-end in the manner illustrated.
2 Each spelling word must be written at least three times and must be spelled correctly.
3 Show an example to get them started.
4 Mount the students' designs and display them attractively.

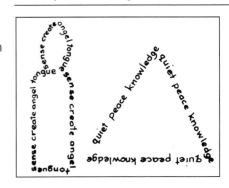

How Many Steps?

This activity can provide an opportunity for a student to practise writing a word in a motivating way.

1 Students use their spelling words to complete a ladder like the one shown, in which each new word must begin with the letter which ends the word before it.
2 They may need to add other words in order to include all the spelling words and complete the ladder.
3 The winner of the game may be the one who has to use the fewest 'extra' words and thereby has the fewest steps.

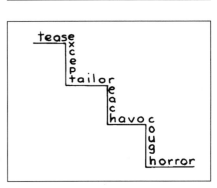

Crazy Words

Show the children some samples of crazy words. When they understand how the 'Crazy Words' work, ask them to create their own. Here are some examples:

Ba na na   Banana split

Dinner
Lunch   Meals on wheels
Wheels

   All   All over the place
the place

<u>ground</u>   Six feet under the ground
feet feet feet feet feet feet

0
B. A.
B. Sc.   Three degrees below zero
M. A.

Rhyming Pairs

Show children an example of a rhyming pair, e.g. a cowardly man (yella fella), then ask them to attempt the following:

a small rodent's home	*(mouse house)*
wet postage	*(damp stamp)*
a distant sun	*(far star)*
a fat baby	*(chubby bubby)*
a bird in a court of law	*(legal eagle)*

Children collect and make up examples for a class book.

Note: When children make up their own rhyming pairs, have them think of pairs first, then develop clues.

Riddle-me rees

Teach children to make up riddle-me-rees like the following:

Clue

It's got four legs.

My first is in *dog* but not in *log*,
My second's the letter between 'h' and 'j',
My third is in *bang* but not in *bag*,
My fourth is in *green* and *magic* and *huge*,
My fifth is a vowel in *owl,*
My whole is something that howls in the night.

Answer: **Dingo**

Note
Discuss the different clues
Line 1 – only one letter different
Line 2 – a good stop-gap
Line 3 – there is only one extra letter added
Line 4 – only one letter in common
Line 5 – could be the first vowel in *outside*, or the second vowel in *below*

Clue

It can swim like a fish.

My first is in *door* but not in *floor*.
My second is in *octopus* and *orange* and *out*.
My third is in *late* but not in *gate*.
My fourth is the letter after 'N' and before 'Q'.
My fifth is the second letter in *this*.
My sixth is in *pick* and also in *fig*.
My seventh is the fourteenth letter of the alphabet
My whole is something that swims in the sea.

Answer: **Dolphin**

Record Keeping

To make a permanent collection of some of these activities the children could have a word study book. A page on synonyms, for example, might look like this:

Warm is a synonym for **Hot**
Wet is a synonym for **Damp**

A **Synonym** is

_____
_____
_____

My favourite synonyms are ...

_____
_____
_____

Extension Activities

There are many children's books available through book clubs, newsagents and department stores that include a variety of similar and other word study activities.

Proof Reading

Proof reading is an important skill that requires intensive teaching. Here is one suggestion for teaching this skill.

Teach children that when proof reading and editing they must ask themselves:

- Have I checked for spelling mistakes?
- Have I checked the punctuation and capital letters?
- Does my writing make sense? Are there any missing words?
- Is there a better way to write it? Could I use more descriptive words? Could I combine two or three sentences into a more interesting sentence? Have I varied sentence beginnings?

Encourage children to develop this checklist through modelling and discussion. The value of this is that children have then thought about, discussed and made decisions about the factors they feel need attention. Write and photocopy the list. Demonstrate how to underline or circle words or elements that need further consideration.

Attach the list to the children's writing folders or desks.

The following activities help children focus on, and develop, proof reading skills. Further suggestions about proof reading are offered on pages 63, 83 and 102 of the *Spelling: Developmental Continuum*.

Proof Reading Activity

1 Select a piece of child's writing.
2 Blackboard a small section of writing from a child's work.
3 Tell the class that you are using the writing sample to teach proof reading skills, but as there were not enough errors you have added some more. This avoids any embarrassment that may be caused as no one, not even the author, knows which errors have been deliberately made by the teacher.

4 If you are working with weak spellers, tell them how many spelling errors there are. Weak spellers have a tendency to mark far too many words as wrong. Also, tell them that every word that is spelled wrongly also appears correctly spelled. They have to decide which one looks right by comparing the two spellings.

Example

The birds were jusst beginning to sing when Kate crept out of bed. 'I wonder if Mum and Dad are awacke yet? I can't hear any noise.'

She krept upstairs. 'I'll take them a cup of tea,' she thought. 'I'll pretend I thort they were awake. I'll just make a little bit of noise accidentally. I wonder where they've hidden my birthday present.'

- Tell the children there are four spelling errors in the piece.
- Ask them to find the incorrectly-spelt words and draw a line under each and write the correct spelling.
- Give the children individual pieces of writing to correct and have them work on selected pieces of their own writing, focusing specifically on proof reading. Insist that any piece of writing brought to you for conferencing or discussion be proof read first.

Dictation Activity

Use dictation of a meaningful passage to provide a context for having-a-go at words, proof reading, teacher modelling and discussion.

Instructions:
- Select a dictation passage which is meaningful to the children i.e. related to a shared experience, class topic/theme, class book.
- Dictate the passage; children write.
- Repeat the passage slowly; children proof read — identify obvious errors (by circling, underlining etc.). Allow students time to:
  try and correct any errors
  write alternative spellings
  choose the version which looks right
- Write the passage on the board modelling 'having-a-go' and other spelling strategies. (This should be done collaboratively with the children).
- Children check their work with the *modelled copy*, circling or underlining any errors. They may then have another go at these words in their 'have-a-go' pad. Some of these words may go into their spelling journal.
- Ask children to do a word count (i.e. check the number of correct words). This would be an optional activity.

Chapter 5:

Assessment and Evaluation

Introduction

Assessment is a process of gathering evidence of students' achievements as writers.
Evaluation is a judgement based on the evidence gained from assessment.

Statement of Principles, Writing K-12, Department of Education, NSW p. 42.

Assessment and evaluation of children's spelling development is viewed within the context of the whole language program. Children's writing is used as a means of gathering information about the child's ability to use standard spelling, experiment with new words, identify words that are non-standard, try alternative spellings, use a variety of strategies when attempting unknown words and proof read their own work.

What Do We Need To Assess?

- Attitude
  enjoyment of writing
  confidence in ability to spell
  development of a 'spelling conscience'
  willingness to experiment with new words
  willingness to check work for standard spelling
  interest in words
- Knowledge
  knowledge of graphophonic relationships
  knowledge of meaning-based relationships
  knowledge of common English letter patterns
  knowledge of different strategies when attempting unknown words
  increasing bank of known words
  knowledge of a process for learning words
- Strategies
  ability to use visual memory to identify non standard words
  ability to identify critical features of words
  ability to make generalisations
  ability to generate alternative versions of words
  development of proof-reading skills

The *Spelling: Developmental Continuum* shows very clearly the behaviours children will be exhibiting at different stages of development. This provides a focus for teacher observation and is an effective method of identifying children's developing knowledge, understanding and skills.

The Continuum provides a moving-on point, a focus for future planning.

Ostrich

They have long legs and it has a long neck and it has feathers. Black feathers and a feathered tail. Big claws and its claw is Black and pink.

(Phonetic Spelling sample)

Last night it was Graduation night. Year 7's item "The nowhere boy" was wonderful. This is the story. Once there was a village of foolish people. Their Queen was Queen Lottie the Lazy. In the village of foolish people there was a gypsy, some copy-cat ministers, a bad boy called Brad and his gang, and, of course Queen Lottie. One day Brad and his (gang) decided to spray the village well. Brad found a spray bottle and graffitied on the well. When Brad was finished he noticed that ...

(Transitional Spelling sample)

How Will Information be Gathered

Through Teacher Observation

The indicators from the *Spelling: Developmental Continuum* provide a focus for observations.

Information can be gathered about:

> what children do when they don't know a word
> their willingness to 'have-a-go'
> strategies used when attempting new words
> willingness to proof read their own work
> use of classroom resources
> interest in words

Analysing Work Samples

Children's work samples can be analysed for information about developing spelling skills. Spelling journals and 'have-a-go' pads also provide evidence of the strategies children are using.

Information can be gathered about:

> the kinds of words the child is attempting
> particular strategies the child is using when attempting words, i.e. phonetic, visual, meaning based
> acquisition of a high frequency vocabulary
> identification of words that are incorrect
> use of varied vocabulary
> use of prefixes and suffixes
> application of generalisations
> understanding of homonyms and homophones
> development of proof-reading skills
> ability to generate alternative spellings

Spelling Conferences

It is important to take time to talk to children about their spelling.

Conferences with each child in the class take place at regular intervals. Some children may need to be conferenced more often and may need frequent help in selecting words to learn for their journal. Through conferences children's needs can be quickly assessed and plans made to support their development. Specific teaching focus groups can be formed on a needs basis within the context of the whole language program.

Children should be encouraged to prepare for a conference by identifying some aspects of their work they are pleased about and some aspect with which they need help.

Self Assessment

Self assessment is an important aspect of evaluation. Children have a good understanding of what they have achieved, what they want to achieve and where they need help. Encouraging children to reflect on how they are going is an important learning experience.

When introducing reflective writing it may be necessary initially to provide some sort of a framework or focus questions to help children with their responses, e.g.
What have I learned this week?
What do I want to learn?
What do I need help with?

Some suggestions about sharing and spelling and reflecting are offered in the *Spelling: Developmental Continuum* Book.

Spelling Interviews

It is worthwhile carrying out specific spelling interviews with children in the class at least once a year. Answers to questions provide useful information about developing attitudes and understandings.

Sample questions and instructions could be:

What do you do if you don't know how to spell a word?
Name someone who is a good speller. Why do you think this?
Why do you think correct spelling is so important in a final copy?
What can *you* do to become a better speller?
If you were giving advice to someone who was having difficulty with spelling what would you say?
What strategies do you use when you are learning a word? How do you go about learning a word?
Write about an interesting word study discovery.

Word Counts

Word counts can be used in the classroom to help all children develop a positive self-image as competent spellers. At least once a month children check samples of their writing to assess their spelling progress. Children count and record the number of words spelled correctly in a first draft or one-off piece of writing. It is important to use a variety of writing forms when taking word counts and to be consistent with the size of the sample taken, e.g. 50 words each time, 100 words each time. Children need to proof read their selection carefully and record the number of *correct* words—it is positive feedback that we are trying to provide.

Scores can be entered on the 'Word Count' record page in a spelling journal so children can monitor their progress.

Parents' Role

It is important to provide parents with information about changes in teaching practice and current practices being used. Information about aspects of the instructional program such as teachers' marking procedures, will help parents understand how children's work is evaluated. The *Spelling: Developmental Continuum* can be used very effectively in an information session to inform parents about children's spelling development in the context of writing. Suggestions can be made as to how parents might support their children's development.

Teachers can also involve parents in the evaluation process by asking them to complete parent information sheets.

Self-Evaluation Sheets

My Spelling Log

What I have learned this week.
I have learned that 'CK' has to have
one or two letters in front.
What I want to learn.
Some more words like 'CK' and
'LL'.
What I am not sure about.
I am not sure about some
Italian words.

An example of a Spelling Log that has been cooperatively devised by children with teacher support. The value of this framework lies in the fact that children have thought about, discussed and made decisions about the factors they feel need attention.

Spelling Progress Card

Name: Class:	Self	Other Student	Teacher	Parent
I have a go at spelling new words.				
I sound out all the parts of a word.				
I make sure the words I spell look right.				
I think of different letter patterns when I'm working out new words.				
I try difficult words again in my 'have-a-go' pad.				
I know how to spell lots of words.				
I use our class word banks and charts to help me to spell.				
I know how to look up words in a dictionary				
I know how to learn a word. ⤙ Look / Cover / Write / Check				
I check my spelling by ticking the parts of the word I've got right and drawing a circle around the hard part of the word.				
I like people to ask me to help them spell a word.				

Parent's signature: ....Date completed ....

Chapter 6:

Helping Children with Spelling Difficulties

Introduction

It is of crucial importance that children's use of words in their writing is not inhibited by their inability to spell. They need a great deal of praise and encouragement to ensure that they continue to have a go and take risks. If children are experiencing problems, it is better to focus on only one word in many different contexts rather than attempting to deal with several at once. Learning will accelerate when children start to experience success.

Suggested Pathway for Intervention

Gather data and plot child on the *Spelling: Developmental Continuum*

Analyse information and identify important teaching strategies according to phase of development

Decide which of the six major aspects of spelling (see next page) should be given extra attention

If more in-depth error analysis is required for older children who are operating largely in the Conventional Phase, refer to Error Analysis Chart and Record Sheet on pages 87–8 of this book.

Six Major Aspects of Spelling

Six major aspects of spelling which may cause problems for children have been identified. These are:

- acquiring a large high frequency vocabulary
- developing graphophonic understandings
- knowledge of common sequential letter patterns
- knowledge of meaning and morphemes
- knowledge of and control over strategies, so that the most appropriate can be applied across a range of contexts.
- breaking away from 'safe' spelling and 'reluctant' writing

Developing a High Frequency Vocabluary

Children need to develop a spelling vocabulary of high frequency, commonly-used sight words. These words make up approximately 50% of what we read and write. If children can spell these words automatically, it will greatly facilitate their writing. If children are having problems with some common high frequency words, it is of fundamental importance that they learn to focus on the critical (most significant) features of a word, e.g. ca**l**m, ca**l**f, wh**a**t. Mnemonics (memory tricks and rules) can be used to help them memorise these critical features.

General Activities

Some suggested activities that will help children learn high frequency words:

- Decorate or illustrate the words.
- Type out the words.
- Look at a word.
  Focus on the part which is causing a problem.
  Shut your eyes.
  Think about the word.
  Write it down.
- Make the words into a crossword puzzle.
- Write the word.
  Think about it.
  Fold the paper over.
  Write the word.
  Check back.
  Correct if necessary.
- Write the word on graph paper.
  Cut the letters out.
  Build the word from the cut-out letters.
- Colour and trace over the word five times.
- Write a nonsense sentence including as many of your spelling words as you can.
- Make a design using the spelling words printed end to end, e.g. a circle, a triangle, a spiral.
- Take one of your spelling words. Make as many other words from it as you can by adding to it and making other words from it, e.g. reference: referenced, referencing, references, referee, referent, refer.

- Write the words using string or pipe cleaners.
- Use spelling words to make a spelling step ladder.
  Each word should start with the letter which ends the word before.
  Other words may need to be added to create links between the spelling words.
- Write out the spelling words leaving out some letters.
  Fill in the missing letters the next day.
- Jumble up the letters of the spelling words.
  Sort them out the next day.
- Find words that rhyme with the spelling words.
  Decide if they are spelled the same or differently.
- Make a grid.
  Insert a friend's spelling words into the grid, either horizontally or vertically.
  Fill the gaps with random letters.
  Challenge the friend to find and circle the words.

Cloze Activities

Cloze activities can be used to focus on high frequency words. Prepare a passage by deleting any high frequency words you want to focus on. Arrange the deleted words from the passage at the top of the sheet for children to select from.

Frame Sentences

Use sentence frames to develop a reading and spelling vocabulary of high frequency, commonly-used sight words. Knowledge of function words can be built up through making up sentence patterns based on concepts, e.g. 'What is round?'
> A ball is round.
> A hoop is round.
> An apple is round.

Sentence frames can be related to themes, e.g. 'Myself'
> I can...
> I like...
> I have...
> I want...

Bingo

Use high frequency words in the traditional game of Bingo.

1 Write the words on the board for the children to look at closely.
2 Cover the words and call them out. Children write their words onto their Bingo cards.
3 Uncover words. Children check their spelling and correct any words incorrectly spelt.
4 Play Bingo.

Word Searches

Select a number of high frequency words to focus on for the week. Children search for these words in magazines, newspapers and teacher prepared text. Children circle or underline the words. At sharing time, the children count up how many words they have found and read out sentences with particular words in them.

Wordbuilding

Ask children to use focus words to build other words, e.g.

'Look at the word *was*; now use it to make other words: ___p, ___n't, ___h, ___te.
'Look at the word *the*; now use it to make other words: ___y, ___re, ___ir, ___n, o___r.
'Look at the word *her*; now use it to make other words: t___e, w___e, ___e.

Shared Book—Poems, Songs, Nursery Rhymes

Focus on high frequency words as a post reading activity, e.g.

- Use 'post it' stickers to cover up high frequency words. Children are asked to come and write the missing words on the blackboard.
- Carry out a 'word search'. Ask the children to see how many *they* words they can find?

Rebus Activity

Prepare a piece of text with pictures for some of the words. Children write out the story replacing the words with pictures.

Hidden Word Puzzles

Children search for hidden words and write them out.

Making Words

Make some new words by writing the letters in the boxes in front of the word 'ant'.

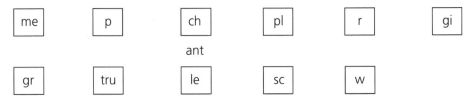

| me | p | ch | pl | r | gi |

ant

| gr | tru | le | sc | w |

If you think a word sounds right, but don't know what it means, try looking it up in your dictionary.

- Now try making a list of all the letters that could go in front of 'all' to make new words.
- Can you think of another small word you could play with in this way?
- How many words can you think of that have 'the' in the middle or at the beginning?

Children can also construct words by combining individual letters or groups of letters with a common letter pattern such as 'ew', 'ain' or 'ion'.

Word Quiz

Look carefully at the following words:
there, time, money, because, heard
Write the word ending in <u>me</u> _____
Write the word with <u>one</u> in the middle _____
Write the word beginning with <u>the</u> _____
Write the word with <u>use</u> on the end _____
Write the word with <u>ear</u> in the middle _____

Developing Graphophonic Understandings

Most children for whom English is the first language gradually make links between symbol and sound as they interact with the written language through their names, environmental print and familiar story books. Letter names provide a natural means of forging these links in the very early stages. It is important that children are given opportunities to think and talk about the links they are making between letters and the sounds they represent. Their contributions should be acknowledged, valued and given a place within the spelling system by charting them and placing the chart in an accessible place as a constant reference point (see examples on pages 36, 52, 71, 91 and 106 of *Spelling: Developmental Continuum*).

It is important that teachers continue to call letters by their names, clearly differentiating between the letter and the variety of sounds that it may represent. Children who may be at risk are in special need of a constant and unchanging 'peg' on which to 'hang' their understandings. The constant factor is the name of the letter which remains the same regardless of the sounds it represents.

Children for whom English is a second language may not be able to 'hear' the sounds of a segmented English word. These children, together with those first language is English but who have not yet developed functional graphophonic understandings, may need to rely on visual strategies in the early stages of learning to read. Teachers can therefore employ a two-pronged strategy. One element of the strategy is to build on the children's strengths and help them further develop their visual memory of words. The other element is to foster graphophonic understandings in the context of their successful learning of visual patterns.

Common Graphophonic Relationships

Consonants: b, c, d, f, g, h, j, k, l, m, n, p, q, r, s, t, v, w, x, y, z

Consonant Clusters:

l as second letter		*r* as second letter			*s* as first letter				Others
bl	gl	br	fr	tr	sc	sp	sl	sn	dw
cl	pl	cr	gr		sch	spl	st	sw	tw
fl	sl	dr	pr		scr	spr	sm		
	sk	squ	str						

Silent Letters   **Digraphs**

bh	mn	gn	ch	th
dh	pn	wr	ph	wh
gh	ps	kn	sh	

Lax Vowels (Short)

h**i**s	m**e**n	h**a**d	**o**ld	h**u**ts

Tense Vowels (Long)

i consonant **e**	ie	y	igh			r**i**de
e consonant **e**	ea	ee	y	ey		th**e**se
a consonant **e**	ai	ay	eigh			l**a**nes
o consonant **e**	oa	oe	ow			**o**ver
u consonant **e**	ew	ue	ui	oo		d**u**nes

Other Vowel Sounds – Vowel Digraphs:

t**oy**	fl**ow**ers	**are**	f**ir**m		**orders**	
oy	ow	ar	er		or	augh
oi	ou		ir		aw	a(ll)
			ur		au	a(lk)

Adapted by permission, from Latham, R. & Sloan, P. (1979), *A Modern View of Reading*, Nelson Australia.

This table of letter/sound relationships can be used by the teacher in conjunction with the class wall chart and the children's own learning journals to determine which graphophonic element should be focused upon. Further information about common letter patterns representing different sounds and different letter patterns which represent the same sound can be found in Appendix 1 on pages 94–102.

Try the following activities to strengthen children's knowledge of graphophonics.

Order of Sounds

- Teach children to listen to the order of sounds in a word and represent these with a letter or letters in correct sequence.
  Sound frames can be used to assist children to identify the place of individual letters within a word. If a child asks for the spelling of jumped, the teacher might prepare a frame to help the child fill in as many letters as possible, J U M P E D.

- Reinforce the understanding that letter-sound correlation is different in different words. Re-teach the concept that:
    - one letter can represent a number of sounds, e.g. 'a': cat, able, car. probable, apparent, father, any
    - the same sound can be represented by different letters, e.g. sound 'lay': ate, ray, rain, obey, steak, veil, gauge, reign.

- Reinforce the understanding that sounds need to be represented by one or more letters. If letter frames are set up for words (as shown in 'Order of Sounds' on previous page), the following questions can be asked:
    - What is the very first sound you hear?
    - Do you know what letter can be used for that sound?
    - In which box do you think it should be written?

  Parts of syllables can be taught in a similar manner. this shows children that the parts must occur in the correct sequence

  (Judith Rivalland, Edith Cowan University)

What Comes Next?

The game '*What Comes Next?*', which is described in the Word Study section on page 54 of this book, provides children with excellent opportunities to focus on graphophonic relationships, particularly when the chosen word is one which is familiar to the children. This game can be played with the whole class as it will enable all children to further their understandings of the spelling system whatever their level of development. Lists of possible letter combinations, the 'could be' lists, can be explored when the game has been played several times with a focus on a particular set of letters, so that children can construct rules about letters and letter patterns and the sounds they represent.

Word Sorts

Children need opportunities to take part in both *Open* and *Closed Word Sorts* as described in the Word Study chapter on page 54 of this book. Words sorted by the children should be drawn from their bank of known words, as their familiarity will make it easier for children to make connections between known letters and letter combinations and the sounds of the words.

Word Snakes and How Many Steps?

These games, which are described on pages 62 and 65, can also be used to explore symbol/sound relationships. The essence of each game is to join one word to another by matching the final letter of one word with the initial letter of the next. Children can be challenged to discover whether the two letters sound the same or different in the two words, e.g. hopot (hop/pot) where the letters represent the same sound and wasit (was/sit) where the same letter represents different sounds. Children could use red and blue circles to note the differences. Children may need support as they attempt this task. Once they become confident they can be further challenged to go on a 'Word Hunt' and find other words which contain letters representing one sound or the other, e.g. was/is/his/nose/dogs - sit/sad/past/us/sing.

Alphabet Activities

Different types of alphabet books can be constructed.

Children can make up their own alphabet books, which they can illustrate and use themselves or donate to younger children.

An alphabet book could become a personal dictionary in which children can write words which they know or want to learn.

Children could be challenged to make an alphabet book which contains two examples of each way a sound can be represented by the same letter, for instance: cat/come, circle/Cynthia, church/chair, Christmas/chemist. They might take a long time to discover and collect examples, but this can be an on-going activity.

Children can cooperatively compose alphabet rhymes, such as:

A is for apple and Astrid and at
B is for Bernard and baby and bat
C is for Catherine and cosy and cab
D is for Dennis and dirty and dab
E is for early and even and eat
F is for forty and Francis and feet
G is for Gareth and golden and got
H is for hero and happy and hot
I is for icy and Ivan and inks
J is for Jasmine and Joseph and jinks
K is for Katie and Kenneth and keen
L is for Lesley and litre and lean
M is for Martin and Mary and main
N is for Nicholas and for Norraine
O is for opal and orange and out
P is for Penny and Peter and pout
Q is for quarter and quiet and quip
R is for Rosemary, Raelene and rip
S is for Sharon and sister and stop
T is for tiny, Theresa and top
U's for umbrella and ugly and umpire
V is for Vincent and also for vampire
W is for William and washing and wrecks
X is for nothing but X-ray and X
Y is for yesterday, yellow and you
Z is for zany and zebra and zoo

  or

A acts angrily
B bounces back
C creates chaos
D dreams dangerously
E eats elephants
F fancies fruit
G grabs grapefruit
H has horses
I interprets Italian
J enJoys jokes
K keeps knick-knacks
L likes leopards
M moves mountains
N nags neighbours
O opts out

83

P prefers photos
Q quits quietly
R roars rudely
S sharpens scissors
T tells tales
U upsets unicorns
V values vampires
W wails wearily
X eXpells eXperts
Y yells yahoo
Z zaps zips

Children can be encouraged to use their dictionaries, their parents and any other resource to find unusual and zany words.

Strengthening Knowledge of Common Sequential Letter Patterns

Children need to understand that words must not only *sound* right, but they must also *look* right.

Some children seem to get 'stuck' in the Phonetic Phase of spelling development. These children usually have a sound understanding of graphophonic relationships but have not developed any alternative strategies that they can apply when a graphophonic strategy is not appropriate. One of the major strategies they need to develop is the use of common letter patterns which characterise the spelling of English words.

Children need to be taught to look for and focus on the highly predictable sequential letter patterns of English.

Word sorting and categorising are important activities in developing this skill. Praise children who identify patterns in new words. Add these to any pattern lists you have around the room. Help children to look for the common patterns in words. Encourage children to mark the patterns, e.g. n**ee**d, f**ee**d, s**ee**d and group words which contain common patterns, e.g. **other**, br**other**, m**other**, b**other**

Encourage children to use trial and error. When they feel a word does not look right they can test and experiment with possible alternatives, until they think it looks right. Model this for them on the blackboard.

The two activities which offer the greatest help to children who need special help in this area can be found in the Word Study section of this book. They are:

What Comes Next? (page 54)
This game should be played systematically every day, focusing on specific patterns which are giving trouble.

Open and Closed Word Sorts (page 55)
Sorting activities can feature words which exhibit the same patterns, although they may be pronounced differently, and different patterns which represent the same sound.

Further Activities

Encourage children to:

- Carry out the activities described in the section 'Teaching Children Spelling Strategies' on pages 8 to 10, with particular emphasis on (iii) Fill the Gap.
- Try the General Activities provided in the 'Developing a High Frequency Vocabulary' section on page 77 of this chapter.

Developing Knowledge of Meaning and Morphemes

Children experiencing difficulties often forget that meaning can be a guide to the spelling of words. In English most words that have the same meaning-base are spelt the same. If the meaning is different then the spelling is different. The way the word is written reflects meaning. In this way we can go straight to the deep structure or meaning of written texts without sounding-out the words. For example, sign and signature have related spellings and related meanings, while seen and scenery have different meanings and different spellings.

This knowledge of the structure of words and the meaning-function of different parts of words can greatly help children learn to spell. For example, the following are all the past tense of verbs:
- want-**ed**/sounds **id**
- bang-**ed**/sounds **d**
- pick-**ed**/sounds **t**

The common element is **-ed**, which signals the past tense. Teaching children to explore and understand word meanings and derivations will help them to become more effective spellers.

Morphemes are units of meaning. Dissolve contains two morphemes **dis** and **solve**, and thus has a double 's'. Disappear only has one 's' because the two morphemes are **dis** and **appear**.

Teaching children to use morphemic knowledge will also help them to recall spelling.

Try the following:
- Ask students to collect as many words as they can with a specific prefix, e.g. 'un'. From the evidence they have collected, challenge them to define the meaning of the prefix.
- Challenge students to choose another prefix which they encounter in their reading, and discover its meaning in the same way.
- Ask the students if they think they can do the same thing with a suffix. Challenge them to provide evidence in support of their statement.
- Challenge students to see how many words they can construct from any one morpheme, e.g. build, built, building, builder, builds.
- Encourage students to choose one Latin or Greek derivative and find as many words using that derivative as possible, e.g. primas: primacy, prima donna, primarily, primary, primate, prime, primer, primeval... or quart: quarter, quartet, quartz...
- Give students one stem from which they can build as many words as possible, e.g. rest: restful, restive, restless, restaurant, restitution, restore, restrain, restrict...
- Ask students to find as many compound words as possible. Let them divide these into their component parts and print them on cards while younger children can then use to play snap, e.g. foot/ball, pea/nut etc.

85

The discovery of word derivations can also guide spelling,e.g. **graph**ics, **graph**ology, tele**graph**; **sign**, **sign**al, **sign**ature, re**sign**; **histo**ry, **histo**rian, **histo**rical.

Developing Knowledge of and Control Over Strategies

Children need to learn to use a range of different spelling strategies and techniques according to the demands of the task. If the use and application of specific strategies is discussed in context and children are praised for applying them, then they will become consciously aware both of the range of strategies and of their need to apply the most appropriate strategy in a given context. This conscious knowledge gives a child control over her or his learning. It also enables a speller to diagnose accurately those areas in which he or she needs additional support. Major strategies are:

* using graphophonic knowledge
* using knowledge of common letter patterns
* using visual memory
* using meaning and morphological knowledge
* consulting an authority

Making strategies explicit

Children experiencing difficulties need to *know that they know* how to approach a problem. As strategies are taught children can be given, or, better still, create their own, prompt cards to remind them what to do. Some examples are shown in Appendix 4 on page 108.

Spelling Error Analysis Chart

The chart on page 87 can be used to analyse the errors made by children in upper primary whom we might expect to spell conventionally on most occasions. Teachers can establish the categories of errors made by children in their writing, and then decide on strategies to help overcome these errors.

Record Keeping

Teachers may find that the record sheets on pages 88–9 will provide them with a clear and systematic means of focusing on the progress of students who are experiencing difficulties. Record-keeping can then be directly linked to the explicit teaching activities and strategies outlined in this chapter. It is not necessary to keep such detailed records of the progress of most students.

Spelling Error Analysis Chart

(Reprinted with permission from CATCHWORDS ((1983)) by M. Peters and C. Cripps. Copyright © by Harcourt, Brace and Company, Publishers.)

Types of Errors	Examples	Possible Teaching Strategies
Reasonable phonic alternatives as well as homophones	**where** for **wear** **hoaped** for **hoped** **sed** for **said** **tort** for **taught** **wite** for **white**	These errors conform to English spelling patterns. If the teacher keeps children involved the errors will gradually disappear. Correction can focus on the critical features where the mistake occurs and the correct letter pattern can be provided ar ir e.g. grammer berd
Errors with sequential letter patterns in English and reversal of digraphs	**sok** for **sock** **happe** for **happy** **siad** for **said** **rihgt** for **right** **stashun** for **station**	These words may appear to be reasonable phonic alternatives. However children who are making these errors have not learned about sequential letter patterns in English. We need to talk to them about the patterns of English and encourage them to look for other words with similar patterns. Emphasise the letter patterns in words rather than the sounds in words, e.g. **rough, tough, through, flower, power, flow, prow, cow.**
Inability to hear sounds in sequence, incorrect articulation, reversal of phonemes	**spay** for **spray** **wif** for **with** **poud** for **pound** **fan** for **van** **gotta** for **got to**	You may wish to check children's articulation and hearing. Encourage children to use visual imagery, to look for patterns in words and focus on critical features. Write words down when children ask for help. Focus on morphemes.
Errors associated with the meaning system	not knowing common morphemes, e.g. **com**; **tele**; **un**; **dis**; or word endings, e.g. **tion**; **ing**; **ment**	Focus on suffixes and prefixes. Teach root words, derivation of words and morphological knowledge.
Reversal and persevertion errors (repetition of parts of words)	**dad** for **bad** **sab** for **sap** **everery** for **every**	Focus on the way children form letters. Try to watch the children in process as they write. Encourage correct letter formation.
Unclassified errors	errors which show wild guessing and little knowledge of spelling system, e.g. dragas for dangerous	Children making these errors have not come to grips with the systematic nature of spelling. Try to build up confidence. Keep a word bank of the words the child does know. Begin with words which will be personally meaningful to the child. Point out letter strings and letter sequences. Do word counts and word sorting.

Example of Individual Record Sheet

NAME				
Strategies and Skill	**Date**	**Date**	**Date**	**Date**
1 Increasing high frequency vocabulary				
2 Increasing graphophonic understandings: Representing some sounds with symbols				
Representing most sounds with symbols				
Representing sounds in correct sequence				
Using reasonable phonic alternatives				
3 Increasing knowledge of common sequential letter patterns				
Can tell if a word does not look right				
4 Using meaning strategies				
Using knowledge of morphemes				
5 Can talk about strategies used				
6 Is taking risks and 'having-a-go' at new words				

Example of Group Record Sheet

SPELLING GROUP	Reasonable phonic alternatives	Errors with sequential letter patterns	Errors with hearing sounds in sequence	Reversal and perseveration errors	Errors associated with meaning	Unclassified errors
Name of Child						

Breaking Away from 'Safe' Spelling and 'Reluctant' Writing

Children need to participate in authentic writing activities where they are writing for real audiences and purposes across the curriculum. Children who could be described as 'reluctant writers' or 'safe spellers' will need specific support to encourage them to have a go at new words and use more varied vocabulary. The following teaching strategies have proved to be very effective in developing interest in writing and increasing output.

Teacher Modelling of Writing Tasks

Teacher modelling of different writing tasks helps children to understand the decisions writers make during the writing process. As teachers 'think aloud' they demonstrate risk taking with language usage, i.e. having a go at new words, thinking of alternative words and phrases and trying ideas. It is important for teachers to model different aspects of the writing process for children, e.g.

- pre-writing strategies
- beginnings, conclusions
- adding detail
- developing ideas
- changing words or phrases
- deleting unnecessary information
- spelling strategies
- proof reading strategies

Collaborative Writing

This may involve the teacher in jointly composing text with either the whole class or a small group. Alternatively children can work collaboratively with a writing partner. Collaborative writing enables children to be involved in the writing process without having to carry the full responsibility for composition.

Writing Across the Curriculum

As children write in different curriculum areas for different purposes they will naturally use more varied vocabulary. For example, before writing in Social Studies or Science, children may be involved in reading, talking, sharing personal knowledge, brainstorming, developing semantic grids or word maps. This helps develop familiarity with concepts and provides children with appropriate vocabulary for their writing task. 'Safe spellers' are more likely to take risks with the spelling of a particular word they need to use to convey precise meaning in writing tasks such as:

- writing instructions
- maths summaries
- science reports
- note taking for research topics
- minutes for class meetings
- letters to the editor
- scripts for news broadcasts
- personal learning logs

Text Innovation

Text innovation involves children in using a familiar text structure as a framework for their own writing. This kind of support enables children who are having difficulty with writing to experience success as they compose their own versions. Children may innovate on a text structure by:

- changing words or phrases
- changing characters
- adding characters
- deleting characters
- changing beginnings or endings
- expanding stories
- developing further tales

Read and Retell

The 'read and retell' strategy as described by Hazel Brown and Brian Cambourne in their book *Read and Retell* is an effective strategy for 'safe spellers' and 'reluctant writers'. It focuses children on meaning as they are involved in predicting, sharing, listening, justifying, reading and writing. It has been found that one of the most important effects of the retelling procedure is the 'almost unconscious learning of text structures, vocabulary and conventions of written language taking place'. (Brown and Cambourne, 1987, *Read and Retell*, page 10.)

Retelling procedures can be varied to accommodate different levels of language ability. There are different forms of retelling procedure, e.g.

- oral to oral retelling
- oral to written
- oral to drawing
- written to oral
- written to written
- written to drawing
- diagram to oral or written
- drama to written
- written to drama

Readers Theatre

'Readers Theatre' provides writers with the opportunity to manipulate language as they develop a play script from a narrative text. Before children become involved in developing their own scripts they need to become thoroughly familiar with the features of play scripts (e.g. through play reading or orchestrating poems). The next step is to involve the class in a collaborative writing activity where teacher and children work together on developing a script from a familiar text. This may then lead to some small group work where children work on composing texts together.

Circle Stories

Circle stories is another variation of cooperative story making that can be used very effectively to support 'reluctant writers' and 'safe spellers'.

The technique involves children in creating stories, by taking turns to build onto a story. The strategy is introduced through involving children in retelling known stories. Once children are familiar with the procedure, spontaneous story making can be attempted. The strategy is most successful when implemented with small groups.

91

The teacher can provide a focus for the story telling. Children sit in a small circle and when the 'story stick' is handed to them they tell the next part of the story. Following this oral activity children may choose to write their own related story or present the story as a class 'Big Book'.

Sharing Writing

All children need the opportunity to share their writing with other children in the class. When children join a 'writers circle' they are encouraged to discuss any problems they are having or identify aspects of their work they are pleased with. It can be useful at times to have a focus for the sharing session, e.g. 'This week we are looking at character descriptions'. Small group sharing is preferable as more children have the opportunity to contribute, however, there will be times when teachers want all children in the class to be exposed to a particular example of writing. It is important to establish requirements for participation in the 'writers circle' such as the need for everyone involved to bring along a piece of writing they want to share. Teacher modelling of the kind of support you want children to give each other is most important. Teacher conferences also provide an opportunity for writers to discuss aspects of their work. Again, it is important for children to be made aware of how they should prepare for a conference, e.g. some teachers prepare a checklist for children or provide them with a focus for their conference.

Playing With Word Activities

Any games that involve children in playing with or manipulating words and building on word knowledge are worthwhile. *Expanding sentence activities* where children use the 'Who, What, Where, When' question word framework to further develop their ideas, are also of value. *Crossword puzzles* really involve children in thinking about word meanings and structures in a very enjoyable way. They are particularly beneficial if they relate to familiar topics, books, characters and events. *Word sorting activities* where children are involved in categorising words help to draw attention to features of word structure and usage.

Activities That Focus on Words in Text

Activities which focus children's attention on particular words in text are also important for developing writers. Cloze passages can be developed to draw attention to particular words. Children read through the text, writing in the words that have been deleted. This is followed by class discussion where children justify their choice of words and make inferences about the author's choices.

Using a 'Have-a-Go' Pad

The introduction of a 'have-a-go' pad can be helpful for writers who are overly concerned with their spelling during the draft writing stage. Children are encouraged to 'have-a-go' at unknown words while writing their first drafts and then later in the process tackle the words again, in their 'have-a-go' pads. This approach reinforces the understanding that there will be words they are not sure of, but these can be dealt with during proof reading.

Use of Resources

All children need to be familiar with resources that can help them with word usage and spelling in their writing. They need to be taught the skills that will enable them to use these resources effectively. Teacher modelling of use of dictionaries and thesauruses during the writing process will help children to understand that *all* writers make use of these resources.

Lots of Reading

As children are reading, or being read to, they are internalising language structure, vocabulary and use of conventions. They are developing knowledge and understanding of language use that they will use in their own writing. It is important to ensure that all children have the opportunity to read for enjoyment every day and listen to the teacher reading from a range of texts.

Self-Evaluation

The involvement of children in self-evaluation helps them develop control over their own learning. Children can be asked to write about an aspect of their work they are pleased with or something they want to improve. Following this they may be involved in goal setting where they identify goals they would like to achieve over a period of time.

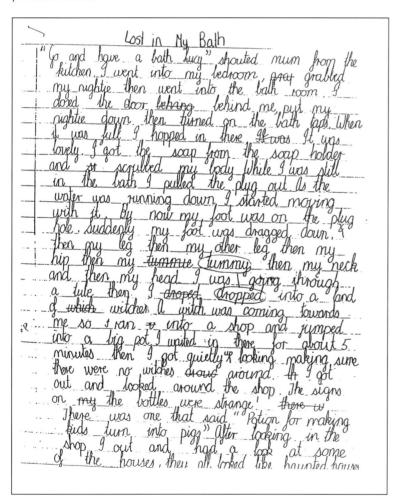

Independent Spelling sample

Appendix 1: An Overview of Graphophonic Elements

The following pages contain:

- a list of common visual patterns and
- a list of different spellings for the same sounds.

These may be useful for teachers when planning, post-programming or recording children's progress. It is not expected that children will learn the patterns in the order presented, or learn a large number at any one time. However, with constant practice at finding patterns and discovering the various sounds that the letter combinations represent, young children will be well on the way to becoming active and independent learners of graphophonics. They will be able to work out rules for themselves and make generalisations about those rules.

There are many contexts that provide a focus for teaching graphophonics. Some contexts are:

- a resource such as a Big Book from which a prominent letter or pattern can be selected;
- daily blackboard news items featuring a letter or letter patterns;
- children's names; or
- a piece of children's writing that shows the use of a letter of the alphabet or a letter pattern.

Be aware that children will not follow a neat order in developing their awareness of symbol/sound relationships. A post-programming approach may be useful for keeping a record of children's learning. Such a record will help in the planning of consolidation activities or the introduction of new symbol/sound relationships.

- When introducing single letters (using letter names and getting children to discover what different sounds the letters can make) it is advisable to begin with those that are visually very different. One such sequence might be:
  s t m b a f c e r o d i h g n y l p u w k v j x z q
- Blends are best practised using puzzles such as 'Secret Messages' (see page 50).
- The words in the following lists contain examples of sounds that the letter patterns represent. It is not intended that they be taught as key words.
- In the 'Some Common Visual Patterns' list digraphs are arranged in approximate order of difficulty from left to right.
- Young children would be unlikely to discover all of these sound/symbol relationships. In the early years only the more obvious relationships will be understood.

Some Common Visual Patterns

Aa	**ay**	**all**	**au**	**ae**
ant angel bath swan address water	hay quay **ai** paid plait captain said **ar** car wart scarce	tall tally **a-e** cake mare delicate **air** chair **are** square	haunt sausage **aw** claw **al** walk palm halt	aeroplane aesthetic archaeologist **aigh** straight **augh** laugh daughter
Bb bat thumb	**bb** rabbit			
Cc cat city electrician scent	**ch** chin chemist machine sandwich	**ck** snack	**cc** eccentric tobacco	
Dd dog soldier	**dd** fiddle	**dge** bridge	**ed** caged landed jumped	

Ee red evil sesame house	**ee** geese **ea** eagle bread break cereal sergeant **ear** pear hear pearl heart **er** jerk mother	**eer** deer **ey** key prey **ew** chew sew **e-e** athlete fete	**ei** their ceiling rein weird forfeit **eo** people dungeon geography video **el** snorkel **eau** beautiful beau	**eu** amateur feud **eous** hideous righteous **eigh** weigh height **eign** foreign reign
Ff fly of	**ff** coffee			
Gg grass giant mirage gnat design	**gg** trigger	**ght** sight	**gu** guest penguin guru	
Hh hat ghost honest				

Ii ink pilot ski	**I-e** ride recipe give trampoline **ing** king stingy dinghy **ir** girl	**igh** high **ie** pie chief friend obedient society soldier **ier** fierce premier	**io** million violent **ior** senior **ia** trial diamond aviator media	**ious** serious precious **ise** advise practise **iour** behaviour **ine** engine fine **ign** malign malignant
Jj jar				
Kk kangaroo knight				
Ll lace palm	**ll** pallet	**ly** kindly	**le** knuckle	**el** snorkel
Mm jam mnemonic	**mm** hammer			
Nn nail think	**nn** thinner **ng** strong	**ngth** strength		

Oo orange honey oval do	**oo** book moon blood **ow** cow show **oa** boat **oy** toy	**o-e** bone glove prove pore **oar** boar **or** cork worm tractor **oi** point choir tortoise reservoir	**oor** poor **ou** cloud soup country course courteous **oul** should shoulder **oe** canoe hoe amoeba	**our** hour journey odour pour **ough** rough drought fought cough dough through thorough **ous** enormous
Pp pancake pneumonia	**pp** slipper	**ph** phone		
Qq Iraq	**qu** queen bouquet queue			
Rr red mother	**ee** hurry purr	**re** centre respond redo		
Ss sand was sugar treasure isle	**ss** kiss session **sh** shop	**sch** school schedule **tch** witch	**sc** scent conscious scarf **sion** revision	**shion** cushion

Tt table nature listen impatient	**th** thick mother thyme **tt** butter		**tion** question position bastion	**tious** ambitious
Uu umbrella unicorn push crusade	**ur** church	**u-e** amuse capture sure	**ue** glue duel guest plaque Tuesday	**ui** guide guitar suite fruit anguish **ua** guard gradual persuade language suave
Vv van	**vv** skivvy			
Ww wet wrinkle	**wh** whip			
Xx extra xylophone example				
Yy yawn cry cylinder crazy martyr				
Zz zebra azure	**zz** buzzard			

Some Different Spellings for the Same Sounds

Variations in speech may affect the way these words are pronounced.

pronounced ar as in jar		**pronounced or as in port**	
far	guard	corn	door
heart	are	jaw	four
clerk	calf	haul	warm
aunt	bath	caught	ball
	roar	bought	
	sore	talk	

pronounced ur as in fur		**pronounced oy as in boy**
curl	work	joy
her	were	coin
bird		
learn		

pronounced oo as in zoo		**pronounced oo as in cook**
do	crew	good
shoe	flute	wolf
move	blue	put
soup	slueth	could
fruit	truth	

pronounced ow as in cow	**pronounced air as in fair**	
now	pair	bear
loud	care	scare
plough	there	
	their	

pronounced ear as in hear	**pronounced f as in fall**
beard	fin
here	photograph
jeer	laugh
fierce	coffee
weir	

pronounced ay as in hay		pronounced a as in hat
hay	straight	pat
nail	vein	plait
gate	baby	
eight	grey	
break	crepe	

pronounced ea as in pea		pronounced e as in pet
tea	key	jet
seed	ski	head
me	chief	said
theme	receive	friend

pronounced i as in ride		pronounced i as in did	
hide	high	pin	busy
find	height	build	women
pie	buy	myth	
my	dye	pretty	

pronounced o as in rode		pronounced o as in dog
rose	dough	job
go	sew	wash
road	brooch	what
low	soul	squash
hoe		cough

pronounced u as in tube	pronounced u as in cup
tune	run
new	son
feud	flood
cue	touch
Hugh	
view	

pronounced j as in jet	pronounced z as in zoo
joke bridge gentle giant soldier	zero is please busy eggs ladies
pronounced ch as in cheese	**pronounced k as in king**
chin catch picture righteous	key come duck chorus bouquet
pronounced s as in sun	**pronounced sh as in ship**
seal cent scene glass	shore sure attention Asia initiate machine issue

Appendix 2: Constructing Rules

Some rules that children can construct for themselves are listed below. Do not tell children the rules. Instead, challenge them to find the answer to a specific question by collecting as many examples as possible, examining the evidence and deriving a rule.

For instance:

- What happens to a 'y' at the end of a word when the word is extended?
  If a word ends in a consonant followed by 'y', change the 'y' to 'i' before adding any ending except 'ing' (silly - silliness, happy - happiness, messy - messier, carry - carriage, hurry - hurried, pony - ponies).
- What happens to a final consonant when a word is extended?
  Words which end in a single consonant preceded by a single vowel double the consonant when you add an ending (plan - planned, begin - beginning)
- What happens when you make a word ending in 's' plural?
  If a word ends with 's', 'sh', 'ch', 'x', or 'z', then you add 'es' (kiss, bus, flash, march, box, fizz).

Make sure that the lists of words children have collected are displayed in a prominent place so that everyone can discuss them. When someone suggests a rule, pin it up beside the list. The rule may not always be accurate or adequate, but leave it until the collection of further evidence enables children to alter or amend it. Only start a search for a rule when a specific query has arisen. Do not try to discover more than one or two rules a term.

The following rules are offered as a collection of examples that may be useful when the occasion arises.

1   *Plurals*

- Add an 's' to most regular words *(tables, chairs)*.
- If a word ends with 's', 'sh', 'ch', 'x', or 'z', then 'es' is added *(kiss, bus, flash, march, box, fizz)*.
- Words that end in a consonant followed by 'o' have 'es' added to them *(mango, tomato)*, although there are exceptions to this rule *(piano, rhino)*.
- In words that end with one 'f', change the 'f' to 'v' before adding 'es' *(half, calf)*. There are some exceptions to this rule *(reef)*.

2   *Consonants*

- Double 'l', 'f', or 's' after a single short vowel at the end of a word; for example, *call, tall, stuff, moss, less* (exceptions: *us, bus, gas, if, of, this, yes, plus, nil, pal*).
- 'k' goes in front of 'e' *(keg)* and 'i' *(kick)*.
- When 'c' goes in front of   'a' *(cat)* or
                                     'o' *(cot)* or
                                     'u' *(cut)*
  it is a hard 'c' which sounds like a 'k'.
- When 'c' is followed by 'e', 'i', or 'y' it sounds like 's', e.g. *centre, circus, cyst*.
- When 'c' is followed by 'h' it nearly always sounds as it does in *church*. Sometimes, however, it sounds like 'k' *(chemist, Christmas)*.
- 'ck' is only used after a short vowel sound *(sack, brick, locket, cricket)*.
- 'q' is always followed by 'u' (except in QANTAS).

- When 'g' is followed by 'e', 'i', or 'y', it sounds like 'j' *(gesture, giant, gypsy)*.
- 'all' and 'well' followed by another syllable have only one 'l' *(already, also, welcome)*.
- No English words end in 'v' or 'j'.
- When 'w' is followed by 'or' it usually says 'wer' *(worst, worm)*. There are some exceptions *(worry, wore)*.
- When 'w' is followed by 'a', the 'a' is hardly ever pronounced as it is in 'apple' *(want, water, wart, wall)*. There are a few exceptions *(wag)*.
- When adding an ending to words with one 'l', double the 'l' *(travel - travelled - travelling, marvel - marvelled)*.
- 'Full' and 'till' joined to another root syllable drop one 'l' *(useful, until, tearful)*.

3   *Vowels*

- the sound 'ee' on the end of a word is nearly always represented by the letter 'y' *(exceptions - committee, coffee)*.
- Omit the final 'e' from a root word before adding an ending that begins with a vowel *(have - having, crave - craving)*. Keep the final 'e' if the ending starts with a consonant *(care - careful, hate - hated)*.
  'E' goes away when 'ing' comes to stay.
- A silent 'e' on the end of a word makes the preceding vowel long (in other words, letter name), for example, *late, bike, cube, bone, scene* (exceptions: *done, come, give, have, love, gone*).
- Drop the final 'e' from a root word before adding an ending beginning with a vowel *(love, loving, lovely, make, making, live, living)*
- 'I' comes before 'e' when it is pronounced 'ee' except when it follows 'e' or is pronounced 'a' - weigh; for example, *brief, field, receive, ceiling* (exceptions: *neither, foreigner, sovereign, seize, counterfeit, leisure, forfeit*).
  'I before E except after C but only when Es are pronounced as in bees'

Appendix 3: Some Latin and Greek Roots

Root word	L = Latin G = Greek	Meaning	Example
accidere	L	happen	accident, decide, incident, decay
ad	L	to	adhesive, adhesion
aequus	L	equal	equality, equal, equator
aer, aeros	G	air	aeroplane, aerial, aeronaut
annus	L	a year	annual, biennial, annals
aqua	L	water	aquarium, aquatic, aqueous
atmos	G	vapour	atmosphere
audire	L	to hear	audible, audience, audition,
auditus	L	hearing	audit, auditorium, auditory
auto-graphos	G	written with one's own hand	autograph, automatic
bene	L	well, good	benevolence, benefactor, benefit
biblion	G	book	Bible, bibliography, bibliomania
bi	G	twice	bicycle, biped, biceps, bicultural
capere	L	to take hold	capable, captive, capacity, accept
caput	L	the head	capital, captain, capitulate
cauda	L	a tail	queue
cedere, cessum	L	to yield, give up	cede, accede, concede, exceed
centum	L	a hundred	centuple, century
circus	L	ring	cycle, bicycle, tricycle, cyclist
civis, civilis	L	citizen	civic, civilised, civilian
claudere	L	shut, close	conclude, exclude, include,
credo	L	I believe	credit, creditor, creed, incredible
decima	L	a tenth	decimal, December, decennial
deka	G	ten	decade, decimal, decagon
dia, metron	G	through, measure	diameter, diametrical
dictatum	L	to say or tell, speak	dictate, dictionary, contradict
ducere, educare	L	to lead, to rear	educate, conduct, deduce, induce
duo	L	two	duet, duologue, duopoly, duotone
elektron	G	amber	electric, electricity, electrical
facere	L	do, to make	factory, fact, office, affect, fashion
ferre	L	to bear, carry	fertile, confer, elate, relate, collate
fluere	L	to flow	fluent, fluid, affluent, influence
frangere	L	to break	infringe, fraction, fracture, frail
fugere	L	to flee	fugitive
fundus	L	the bottom	refund, foundry, confound, fuse

Root word	L = Latin G = Greek	Meaning	Example
ge, logos	G	the earth, a discourse	geology, geography, geometry
glare	G	to freeze	jelly
gradus	L	a step	grade, gradual, ingredient, degree
granum	L	a grain	gram
graphein	G	to write	graph, graphic, autograph,
gratus	L	thankful, pleasure	grateful, disgrace, agree, grace
hydor	G	water	hydrogen, hydrant, hydraulic
jacere, (ejectare)	L	to throw	conjecture, interject, object, eject
jus, dicere	L	to say law	judge, judgement, prejudice
liber	L	free	liberal, liberality, liberate, liberty
logos	G	word, speech	dialogue, monologue, catalogue
magnus	L	great	magnitude, magnify
manus	L	the hand	manacle, manual, manufacture
metron	G	measure	thermometer, barometer, speedometer
migrare	L	to go	migration, immigration, migrant
mikros	G	small	microscope. microphone, micrometer
miles	L	a soldier	military, militia, militant
mille	L	a thousand	millipede, million, millionaire
minuere	L	to lessen	minutes, minuet, miniature, minus
mittere	L	to send	admit, missile, omit, dismiss
monos	G	alone, single	monopoly, monologue, monogram
mors	L	death	mortal, immortal, post-mortem
movere	L	move	motive, motor, commotion, mobile
navis	L	a ship	navy, navigate, navigation
novem	L	nine	November
octo	L	eight	octet
okto	G	eight	octopus, octagon
pathos	G	feeling	pathetic, sympathy, apathy
pars, partis	L	a part of share	partisan, parcel, partner, portion
pes, pedis	L	a foot	pedal, pedestrian, centipede, biped
phone	G	sound	phonic, telephone, phonograph
photos	G	light	photograph, photography
polis	G	a city	metropolis, metropolitan, politics
portare	L	carry, bear	port, porter, portable, export, report
potio	L	a draught	poison, potion
praktikos	G	fit for action	practical
prima	L	first	prime, primitive, primary, premier

Root word	L = Latin G = Greek	Meaning	Example
quattuor	L	four	quadrangle
quintus	L	fifth	quintet
scribere	L	to write	scribe, scribble, manuscript, describe
sentire	L	to perceive, feel, think	scent, sentence, sensible, sense
skopeein	G	to see	telescope, microscope, periscope
septum	L	seven	September
spacere	L	to look	conspicuous, spectacle, suspect
sphaira	G	sphere	spherical, hemisphere
spiro, spire	L	breathe	inspire, expire, expiry, sprite
struere	L	to build	structure
suspicere	L	to look at secretly	suspicious
tele	G	far off, at a distance	telephone, telescope, telegraph
triploos	G	triple	trio, tripod, triplicate
unus	L	one	unit, unity
universus	L	whole	universal
venire	L	to come	convene, intervene, advent, event

Appendix 4: Prompt Cards

Prompt cards are most effective when they are jointly constructed by children and teacher.

If I Can't Spell a Word I Can:

- use my Have-a Go pad and try different letter patterns

- sound it out

- think about the meaning to see if it helps

- divide the word into syllables or into separate parts

- check in my personal dictionary

- look on the charts around the room

- look in our list of class words

- ask a friend

Questions That Will Help Me Work Out How to Spell Words

Does the word look right? If not, have I tried another way to write it?

What is the meaning of the word? Is it like any other word I know?

Do I know where the word comes from?

Can I find the part I'm not sure of and underline it?

Can I divide the word into parts? Have any parts been added to it?

Can I divide the words into syllables?

If I say the word slowly, can I hear the sounds in order?

Have I tried to find the word in a word bank or a dictionary?

Using a Have-a-Go Card

- Think about the meaning of the word. Does it give a clue to the spelling pattern?

- Say the word slowly. Listen to the sounds.

- Write the word syllable by syllable.

- Make sure each sound is represented by a letter or letters.

- Look carefully to see if the pattern looks right, if not:

    - try different patterns that might be right.

    - see if you can think of another word that may be similar. Try again.

How to Learn a Word

- LOOK
  First look at the whole word carefully.
  If there is one part of the word that you find difficult, look specially hard at that part.

- COVER
  Cover the word.

- WRITE
  Write the word from memory.
  Say the word softly as you write it.

- CHECK
  Have you got it right?
  If not, start again — LOOK, COVER, WRITE, CHECK

Proof Reading

Proof reading your own writing is hard because you know it so well. Try to leave it for a few days and then:

- Place a ruler under one line at a time and read each word carefully.

- Circle any words you think are not spelt correctly.

- If you know how to spell any of these words, write the correct spelling above the circle.

- Ask a friend to check that you have circled all the misspelt words.

- Choose up to five of the circled words that you will need to use again in your writing.

- Put these words in your spelling journal and start to learn them.

Acknowledgements

The First Steps *Spelling: Resource Book* has been compiled largely from previous First Steps Modules printed in 1990.

We gratefully acknowledge the contribution made by Dr Bruce Shortland-Jones who has given generously of his time and expertise and Kay Kovalevs for her dedication and hard work in the editing and coordination of the First Steps in the early years of the project.

Bibliography

Brown, H. and Cambourne, B. 1987, *Read and Retell,* Thomas Nelson, Australia, Melbourne, Victoria.

Brown, H. and Mathie, V. 1990. *Inside Whole Language,* Primary English Teaching Association, Rozelle, NSW.

Education Department of South Australia, 1991, *Literacy Assessment in Practice: R-7 Language Arts,* Government Printer, South Australia.

Hill, S. and Hill, T. 1990, *The Collaborative Classroom,* Eleanor Curtain Publishing, South Yarra, Melbourne, Victoria.

Ministry of Education, Western Australia, 1989, *English Language K-7 Syllabus,* State Print, Perth, WA.

Ministry of Education, Western Australia, 1991, *Spelling Developmental Continuum,* State Print, Perth, WA.

NSW Department of Education, 1987, Writing K-12, Sydney.

Ministry of Education, Western Australia, 1987, *Draft Spelling Journal Notes,* State Print, Perth, WA.

Rivalland, J. 1990, *Spelling Zoom Notes,* Ministry of Education, Perth, WA.

Weeks, B. and Leaker, J. 1991, *Managing Literacy Assessment with Young Learners,* Era Publications, Flinders Park, South Australia.